50 MISSION CRUSH

Lt. Col. Donald R. Currier
USAF (Ret)

BURD STREET PRESS

DIVISION OF WHITE MANE PUBLISHING COMPANY, INC.

This Burd Street Press publication
was printed by
Beidel Printing House, Inc.
63 West Burd Street
Shippensburg, PA 17257 USA

In respect for the scholarship contained herein, the acid-free paper used in this book
meets the guidelines for permanence and durability of the Committee on Production
Guidelines for Book Longevity of the Council on Library Resources.

For a complete list of available publications
please write
Burd Street Press
Division of White Mane Publishing Company, Inc.
P.O. Box 152
Shippensburg, PA 17257 USA

Library of Congress Cataloging-in-Publication Data

Currier, Donald R., 1921-
        50 mission crush / Donald R. Currier.
              p.   cm.
        Includes index.
        ISBN 0-942597-43-5
        1. Currier, Donald R., 1921-   .   2. World War, 1939-1945--Aerial
operations, American.   3. World War, 1939-1945--Personal narratives,
American.   4. Navigators--United States--Biography.   5. United
States. Army Air Forces--Biography.   6. B-24 bomber.   I. Title.
II. Title: Fifty mission crush.
D790.c87   1992
940.54'4973--dc20   92-8964
                                                                        CIP

PRINTED IN THE UNITED STATES OF AMERICA

ACKNOWLEDGEMENTS

While this book is a personal account of my war experiences, it could not have been produced without the contributions of many others: first, the surviving members of the crew of the "Wood's Chopper" who lived these events with me; secondly the first hand accounts of the remaining original members of the 718th Squadron, 449th Bomb Group--the "Bruning Bunch"; thirdly, the wartime log of Bombardier Harold Nelson, one of my tent mates.

The Group History in two volumes first published in 1985 and expanded in 1989 was of great value in sharpening my recall of names, places, and actions.

Three women gave me invaluable help on this project. Marty Kumer and Marian Schaller spent many hours going over my early drafts with a fine tooth comb. They forced me to clarify my meanings and pressed me to eliminate much of the jargon of the combat crewman that crept into my story as I got caught up in the memories of those days. My wife, Helen, the girl I called "Blondie", typed the final version of the book and helped with the editing.

One of the most significant contributions to the final product was the work done by George W. Appleby, President of ATMicrosystems, Inc. of Rockville, Maryland. George, using the advanced equipment his company has, organized, then converted my text to camera-ready copy--the final and essential step before printing. Without his effort, this book might not have seen the light of day.

FOREWORD

In today's United States Air Force, any attempt to alter or embellish the official uniform is strictly frowned on. Not so, in our days. The hat we called the "fifty-mission crush" was de rigueur for flight crews. We airmen always wore radio headsets when flying. When the headset was worn over the Army garrison hat, it was necessary that the edges of the hat bend down so that the head phones would fit close to the ears. To do this, veteran flyers took out the grommets that normally stiffened the hat rim. And that's how the "old bold ones" were distinguished from the "new kids"--and also from all of the other Army forces.

CONTENTS

Acknowledgements   iii

Foreword   iv

Illustrations   viii

Introduction   xi

Chapter 1   1
We Get Our Crew Together

Chapter 2   11
We Get Our Own Airplane

Chapter 3   17
We're on Our Way--But To Where?

Chapter 4   25
On To Africa--And Back

Chapter 5   35
We Close In On The War

Chapter 6   45
It's Italy--But Where is Grottaglie?

Chapter 7   **51**
We Set Up Housekeeping-Italian Style

Chapter 8   **59**
Combat! That's What We Came For

Chapter 9   **67**
We Begin To Pay The Price

Chapter 10   **79**
There Is Life After Death

Chapter 11   **85**
We Meet Some of Our Allies

Chapter 12   **91**
The Big Week

Chapter 13   **97**
The "Big Week" Continues

Chapter 14   **105**
March--We're Under The Weather

Chapter 15   **113**
It's April and We're In
The Big Leagues Now

Chapter 16   **123**
   Twenty-five Missions--
   We're Halfway Home

Chapter 17   **133**
   My Faith Looks Up To Thee

Chapter 18   **143**
   We Entertain Some Visitors

Chapter 19   **153**
   It's June and It's Over

Chapter 20   **161**
   We Journey Back to Reality

Chapter 21   **167**
   The Soldier Home From The Wars

Postscript   **171**

Index   **173**

ILLUSTRATIONS

The author at 22.   2
The "fifty-mission crush" was
brand new September, 1943.

The crew of the "Chopper".   14
Topeka, Kansas; December 1943
(Note the nose art.).

First combat loss sustained   68
Mostar, Yugoslavia; January 14, 1944.

Over the ball bearing factory   114
Target at Steyr, Austria; April 2, 1944.

"Ye Old Rugged Curse"   115
Combat artist's depiction of a "heavy"
B-24, fighting her way home from Steyr
on Palm Sunday 1944.

"Wood's Chopper"   132
Sans nose art, May 1944.

Smoke pots   134
Ploesti, Romania; May 5, 1944.

Another look at Ploesti, Romania   135
    June 24, 1944, when strong ground-level
    winds made the smoke pots ineffective.

Precision bombing at its best   144
    Piacenza, Italy; May 12, 1944.

Incredibly accurate enemy flak   145
    Killed author's friend here on his forty-fifth
    mission--Orbatello, Italy; May 17, 1944.

Bombardier's delight   148
    Marseilles, France; May 27, 1944.

Hitting the target Wollersdorf Airdrome   149
    Wiener-Neustadt, Austria, the enemy's
    ME-109 factory and base.

Author's longest mission and fat target   154
    Constanta, Romania; June 11, 1944.

INTRODUCTION

Most Americans know about the air war in Europe during
World War II. The strategic bombing campaign lasted from
late 1942 until the German surrender in May 1945. The
massive aerial attacks over the complete breadth of Europe
from Holland to the Black Sea resulted in the destruction of the
war-making potential of the Nazis--from the factories of
western Europe to the oil fields of Romania--and paved the
way for the successful conclusion of the war in the West.

The United States Army Air Corps was by no means the
only participant in this campaign, nor was the Eighth Air Force
the only American force involved. The Royal Air Force of
Great Britain did great damage to the German heartland by its
massive night bombing raids on the cities and industries of
Germany. And the U. S. Fifteenth Air Force, operating out of
Italy in 1944 and 1945, delivered crushing blows to the underbelly of Germany, the Balkans and, in particular, the oil fields
of Romania.

The key operating philosophy of the American air forces
was daylight bombing using large numbers of heavy bombers
in close formation to deliver massive tonnages of bombs on

targets. It was a dangerous and costly approach, but it greatly improved the accuracy of the bombing over night raids. The losses in planes and crews were enormous by any standard because, while we air crews could see our targets better, the Germans could also see us better. The air battles in the high skies over Europe were epic and will never again be repeated. Fortunately for the air crews of today, nuclear weapons and guided missiles have rendered such combat obsolete.

If one were to ask the average American citizen what kind of airplanes were used in the strategic bombing of Europe, the most likely answer would be the B-17, or "Flying Fortress" as it was popularly called. Almost forgotten would be the B-24 "Liberator" bomber; and yet, much of the bombing of Europe was carried out by the B-24. More of them were built and deployed in Europe than B-17's.

Similarly, the average American would probably overlook completely the role of the Fifteenth Air Force in the air war over Europe; and yet some of the most deadly targets in Europe--the aircraft factories at Regensburg, Wiener-Neustadt, and Vienna; the ball-bearing plants at Steyr; the industrial centers around Budapest and Bucharest; and the vast oil field complex at Ploesti--could only be reached effectively from the air fields of Italy, from whence flew the Fifteenth. The Fifteenth had 3,544 B-24's, as compared to 1,407 B-17's. By May 1945, when operations ceased, 1,756 B-24's and 624 B-17's had been shot down in combat. The B-24 crews shot down 1,374 enemy aircraft and had 505 additional "probables."

How come the B-17 is so well remembered and the B-24 almost forgotten? The B-24 could fly faster, farther, higher, carry a bigger bomb load, and take more punishment than the B-17. The B-24 had a more modern bombsight than the B-17 and had better bombing accuracy. The answer is simple: The B-24 had everything except a good press agent. The B-17 was pretty and sleek--a conventional "tail dragger," whereas the B-24 was ugly, ungainly--sometimes referred to as a "boxcar." It was built to haul bombs, and that's all. It was designed to fly and fight in the incredibly hostile environment of the European skies, and it did that better than any other airplane.

The story of the B-24 and of the Fifteenth Air Force is not unknown to those who truly have been interested in the air war in Europe. There are some good books on those days, and a fine video tape, "The Air War In Europe", narrated by Walter Cronkite, does cover the air operations in the Fifteenth pretty well-especially the Ploesti raids, if you overlook the concentration on the B-17 participation. On the other hand, there aren't too many actual crew stories about B-24 crews who made the missions and came home to tell about it.

Two years ago, I learned that my old group, the 449th Bomb Group, 47th Wing, 15th Air Force, was planning a reunion. At that time, I was indifferent to reunions in general and to a war-time reunion in particular. Forty-one years had passed since those days, and my crew and I had never kept in touch. Further, in the slightly less than six months that I had been flying combat, a majority of my particular friends--the ones I trained with and went overseas with--had been shot down and their places taken by replacements whom I scarcely knew or not at all.

In any event, I sent in my name and address to the reunion secretary, Lt. Col. Dick Downey USAF (Ret), just to get on their roster of 449-ers. Shortly thereafter, I got back from Dick the list of names and addresses that had been found to that date. Going over the list, I found a very few names of guys I vaguely remembered; but there, near the end, was one that made my heart leap--John W. Wood, of Greenville, South Carolina--my pilot.

The last time I had seen John Wood was at Charleston, South Carolina, in October 1944, when he was a check pilot and I was an instructor navigator. We had parted to different lives and never met again nor corresponded. I had no idea what he was now doing nor what his life had been over those forty-one years. I hesitated a long while before writing him a letter, saying only that I saw his name and, if he were interested, I would like to hear from him. Only a few days passed before he replied. We wrote back and forth a few times, and then I called him on the phone. That phone call was one of the most exhilarating things that I can remember, and it set me off on a long search to find out what had happened to the rest of the crew.

Believe it or not, I found and was able to contact six of the original ten guys on our crew. One, our ball turret gunner, "Red" Bauer, was killed in combat when flying with another crew. Our Bombardier, Bob Fenton, had died in 1984 and I learned that Norbert Kneis, our radio operator and nose gunner, had also passed away. I found all of the rest--Wilfred Ayers, Engineer and Top Turret Gunner; Sylvan Lubin, Co-Pilot; Carleton Smith, Waist Gunner; Gilbert Smith, Tail Gunner; Bill Grankowski, Waist Gunner; and of course, John Wood, Pilot. I also located our Crew Chief, Bob Muller--the guy who, as much as anyone, kept us flying.

Talking with these guys after forty-one years, sharing old memories, and recalling names of so many of our comrades who went down in so many battles was a terribly moving experience for me. I wanted to remember more. I was ready to recall what I had long put behind me. I dug out the old letters my Mother and my girl friend--now my wife--had saved for all those years, and the memories came flooding back as if it were only yesterday. I began to tape my memories and to write long letters to the crew asking for details of things that I was hazy about. I contacted fellows from other crews and found out what had happened to many of them whom I last saw going down in flames or bailing out.

John Wood and I decided to go to the reunion and we booked our rooms at the hotel three months in advance of the date to be sure that we would have adjoining rooms. My wife and I stopped to see John and his wife, Ann, for just a night on our way south to visit friends in Georgia in July. John and Ann came up to visit us for three days in August, and we had a great time reliving those wartime days. The reunion was set for October 24-26. On September 16th, I got a call from Ann Wood saying that John had died suddenly of a massive heart attack. Strangely, he was writing me a letter. He had written two paragraphs, finished with a period, and that was it--no sign of distress at all in his writing. Ann sent me the letter, and I still have it.

Helen and I went to the reunion, and we took Ann Wood with us because Ann knew John would have wanted her to go. I saw a lot of my old friends, but I still don't like reunions. I just can't imagine me flying combat, with all those "old" men!

I didn't go to the next reunion and I doubt that I'll ever go again. This book is my tribute to those young men I knew in 1943/44 and to that great airplane, tail number 42-7750, that took us all the way from Bruning, Nebraska, to such exciting places as Regensburg, Munich, Vienna, Bucharest, and Ploesti--and to many other deadly places we didn't even know existed. She brought each of us safely home, day after day, until all of the crew had completed their fifty missions. She "died" one week later, trying to land with a replacement crew after being shot up while bombing an airfield near Budapest, Hungary, on 2 July 1944. There were only three survivors.

CHAPTER 1

We Get Our Crew Together

In the Army Air Corps in World War II, there were two types of training groups —OTU's and RTU's. "OTU" stood for Operational Training Unit and "RTU" stood for Replacement Training Unit. The OTU's were designated bomb groups whose members would not only train together but would be equipped with their own planes, which would take them overseas and would fly together as a unit in combat. The RTU's were assigned to training groups in the States. The crews would train together but would have no operational designation. When finished with their training, RTU crews would be assigned to various combat units to replace lost crews wherever needed. Our crew was assigned to an OTU--the 718th Squadron, 449th Bomb Group.

Having spent a career in the United States Air Force after WW II and seen the high level of training and the skill level of our current combat crews, I can hardly believe how ill-prepared we were to do the job assigned to us. My own case is an example.

1

The author at 22.

I graduated from thirteen weeks of training in navigation school on 11 September 1943. Generously, the Army granted me a 10-day leave, plus three days travel time. That was supposed to get me to Brockton, Massachusetts from Sacramento, California and then to Clovis, New Mexico. And that was train travel since there were no available airline seats for low-priority Second Lieutenants.

To this day, I have no idea why they sent me to Clovis. I was there only four days before being transferred to Bruning, Nebraska which turned out to be the temporary home of the 449th Bomb Group. Arriving at Bruning on the 30th of September, I reported in and was promptly assigned to the 718th Squadron, Crew 8-2-D.

The next day I met my pilot, John W. Wood, who had just been unceremoniously snatched from his hotshot B-26 outfit to become a B-24 driver. He was not the only B-26 pilot to come to the 449th to fill a First Pilot slot, but he was probably the most unhappy of the lot. In those days, as today, "you are what you fly," and a B-24 was nothing but a truck compared to the sleek, fast, and maneuverable twin-engine B-26.

Sometimes there are events in a person's life that turn out to be seminal. I truly believe that I am here to write this tale because of the single fact that I was assigned to John Wood's crew. When I first met John, he was only 20, but already a First Lieutenant. In those days, to be a live pilot of the old version of the Martin Marauder B-26 was a feat in itself. The B-26 pilots trained at McDill Field at Tampa, Florida. The early B-26 had too little wing for its size, and its engines were big, but unreliable. They had a saying at McDill: "A plane a day in Tampa Bay." To have survived training and then flown

3

as an instructor pilot was a tribute to John's surpassing skills as a pilot.

Another factor whose significance I did not appreciate at the time was John's rank as a First Lieutenant. Our squadron commander, Bill Nosker, was only a Captain, and most of the rest of the squadron pilots were brand new Second Lieutenants. John was, therefore, made a Flight Leader, and that had very important connotations when we began flying combat missions.

The 1st of October, 1943 was an eventful day in my life. First, I encountered the toughest guy I had yet to meet. I, along with all of the other officers in the 449th who had so far reported in, were assembled in the base theater that morning for a mandatory formation. On the stage by himself stood our group commander, Colonel Darr H. Alkire. He confronted us with a piercing stare and lo, the place fell as silent as a tomb. When he finally spoke, there was no word of welcome nor even an introduction. There really wasn't any need because we Second Lieutenants recognized God wearing those two eagles on his blouse.

When Colonel Alkire began to speak, his message was direct and to the point. I guess everyone there assembled still recalls his words: "You young punks with that pot metal on your chests think you're pretty hot flyers. Well, you're not! You know nothing about combat flying, but that's what I am here to teach you." Then he got down to business and read us the riot act, scaring the hell out of all of us in the process. He told us what he expected and how unhappy he would be if he didn't get it. He itemized for us a series of fines that would be imposed on any officer who, in any way, screwed up. The fines, depending on the gravity of the sin, could reach $75, which was equal to our monthly flight pay. Father Flannigan's Boys Town, which was in Nebraska, was to be the recipient.

Looking back now, the task Alkire was given by the Air Corps was incredible. We were to be combat trained, fly overseas to Italy, and be ready to fly combat missions in three months. Alkire almost made it, too. The 449th Bomb Group dropped its first live bombs on Mostar, Yugoslavia, on 8 January 1944--just one hundred days after he stood on that theater stage at Bruning. And Alkire, himself, was flying the first plane over the target.

The second great event of 1 October was my first flight with John as Pilot, in an older model B-24-D. This was really nothing but an orientation flight since the rest of our crew was not yet assembled. John was getting flying time to familiarize himself with the airplane. I was along just for the ride. It was my first flight in a B-24, and I was completely amazed by what, to me, was its monstrous size, its four mighty engines, and all of the many instruments on its flight display. Needless to say, I was excited and scared by the thought of my responsibilities to guide such a ship across oceans and deserts and to parts of the world unknown to me. The future seemed a long way from the friendly San Joaquin Valley of California where I had trained as a navigator.

The completion of our crew did not proceed smoothly. Our Co-Pilot, Sylvan Lubin, fresh from flight school, showed up on 6 October. Bob Fenton, our Bombardier, came along at the same time. Our originally assigned Flight Engineer was caught stealing a car and went to jail, and we never got his replacement, Will Ayers, until the 31st of October. Our original Tail Gunner fell off a bomb trailer and fractured his skull, and so we had to shift around the gunner assignments to get a new Waist Gunner. Carleton Smith joined us near the end of October to finally complete the crew.

In the meantime, we were supposedly training seriously for our combat mission. In point of fact, the training was almost exclusively pilot training for the demanding job of high-altitude formation flying. As Navigator, I got in some visual tracking of where we were and had been on those flights, but I never had to guide the plane to any destination. Similarly, Bob Fenton played with his bombsight, synchronizing on various "targets" that passed underneath us. The gunners did nothing. We didn't even carry guns or ammo on the training planes.

All this changed on 12 October. It seems incredible, but the Second Air Force laid on a surprise P.O.M. (Preparation for Overseas Movement) inspection on that day. We, as a group, were briefed to fly a high-altitude bombing mission in formation to northern North Dakota, drop five practice bombs on a range there, fly over to Sioux Falls and make a simulated bombing run on its rail yard and then fly back to Bruning. This, mind you, was just twelve days after we had formed up our group. Further complicating the problem was the weather. It was absolutely terrible with heavy clouds, freezing rain, and near zero visibility. We went anyway, and flying in the right seat with our crew was a Major on the Inspection Team.

The predictable result was a disaster although, miracu-lously, no one got killed. Most of us never saw either the range or Sioux Falls so we dropped no bombs. As the weather worsened, the formation flying fell apart and every plane was on its own. In the next few hours, B-24's from the 449th landed at military and civilian fields all over the Dakotas and Nebraska. Just by sheer luck I found our way home, but we were the only plane in our squadron to make it back that night.

Needless to say, we flunked the P.O.M. and I'm sure Alkire heard some unkind words from the Inspection Team. To put it mildly, he was furious. Once again we assembled at the theater, and he chewed us all up, down, and around and then barked at the hole. He laid on a regimen of high-altitude formation flying that damned near did us all in. Between 13 October and 15 November, the whole group spent nearly as much time above twenty thousand feet as we did on the ground. My records and John's show that we flew ninety hours in thirteen days. Our new combat airplane, 42-7750, arrived on 20 October. By 3 November, we had so much time on her that we had to go back to flying one of the training planes. It was a rule that you could not take off for overseas if you had one hundred hours on the plane because it would require a hundred-hour inspection which was major down time.

We passed the second P.O.M. with flying colors. This was a major event with a capital M, and it required a major celebration by every one of the officers. Most of us hadn't had a drink since the disaster of October 12, so we were ready. Everyone, including Alkire, got drunk and disorderly. Alkire then made a serious professional mistake--he made a pass at the Deputy CO,s wife. Alkire and the Deputy got into a wrestling match but were quickly separated. The party broke up shortly after that.

The next afternoon, all we officers were reconvened in the theater. A contrite Alkire described what happened, pulling no punches. In front of us all, he apologized to his Deputy and the Deputy's wife. Noting that the event had been reported to Second Air Force Headquarters, he said, "It's possible that they may relieve me as Commander of this group. Be that as it may, I'll tell you all one thing. I missed WW-I by a year, and I'm damned if I'm going to miss this one. I'm going with you guys if I have to go as a gunner. You can count on it!"

If any charges were to be brought against Alkire, the bureaucratic process saved him because orders came the next day directing the group overseas. The 449th said goodbye forever to Bruning Army Air Base, departing on 21 November for Topeka, Kansas to stage for the flight overseas. You can guess who was flying the first plane out.

A side note on Alkire: In the late 1950's, I served with a Lt. Col. William Haizlip at Holloman AFB, New Mexico. In fact, we were next-door neighbors in Alamogordo. One night, we were visiting with the Haizlip's and Bill started reminiscing about his early days in the Army when he was an enlisted Crew Chief. This was in the '20's and '30's--from the days of the Barling Bomber. He brought out some old photo albums-- pictures of young Lieutenants and Captains and began telling yarns about them, so fascinating and, in many cases, so hilarious that I will eternally regret not having had a tape recorder with me. Those young "free spirits" with whom he flew became the famous commanders of the Army Air Corps and later the leaders of the fledgling USAF. These guys were the ones that air bases all over the country are named for!

After Bill sort of ran down on his stories, I asked him if he'd ever heard of a Darr Alkire. In his North Carolina drawl he replied, "Shiit, yes! I knew him back in the 30's when he was a Captain. Alkire was a hard-living, hard-drinking son-of-a-bitch in those days. When he was drunk, he was as mean as a snake with a busted fang. He wasn't much better when he was sober. But he was a PILOT!"

I told him some of the stories among us 449-ers about Alkire. Bill laughed.

"That's him to a tee! He hasn't changed a bit!"

CHAPTER 2

We Get Our Own Airplane

We were assigned our new airplane, B-24-H, tail number 42-7750, as I earlier noted, on 20 October, 1944. She was built by Ford at the huge Willow Run plant. Actually, she was assembled there because most of her parts and pieces, except for the airframe, were built elsewhere. She was accepted by the Air Corps on 25 September, 1943. A delivery pilot brought her to Bruning, and she became ours by the luck of the draw.

We had about three weeks of training flights in 42-7750 before we ran out of time on her engines and had to let her sit. She was not without her faults. For example, the turbo super-charger on her No. 4 engine would not work properly and we had a hard time pushing her above nineteen thousand feet. Bob Muller, our Crew Chief, fussed with that thing at Bruning but to no avail. The problem persisted even after we reached Italy. When we were forced to abort a couple of missions because of that, Engineering gave us a new supercharger which cured the problem.

Our problems with 42-7750 continued. On the day the
group was scheduled to depart Bruning for Topeka, Kansas,
Muller discovered that one of the wing gas tanks was leaking.
There was no alternative except to change it. Unfortunately,
the group, including the Engineering section, departed on
schedule leaving us behind.

Muller, who could not draw on the services of other crew
chiefs or of our group maintenance people, had to "draft" us air
crew to assist him. We pitched in trying to help him more than
getting in his way. We could tell that he felt uncomfortable
ordering us officers around, but we knew who the expert was
and didn't mind. Our aim was to shake the dust of Bruning off
our collective feet and get on with the war. We changed the
tank in about eight hours.

Then, everything was back to square one when, on filling
the tanks, we discovered that the replacement tank leaked too!
We had the plane dragged back into the hangar and started all
over again, finishing about 3 A.M. the following day. This
time, no leaks appeared, and we flopped into bed exhausted.
We finally geared up and left Bruning for Topeka on the 23rd
of November.

Looking back, our problem with the tanks was not without
its benefit. When you are in a training squadron, you are
assigned a plane by its tail number. No matter how much you
fly that same plane, you don't have any personal attachment to
it. But, when they give you an airplane and say "this is yours,"
you immediately want to personalize it--to make it distinctive.
You want to christen it and put your own art work on it.
That's how we felt about 42-7750.

12

We had been struggling for a couple of weeks to come up with a meaningful name and design. While we were working on the gas tanks, a guy from the base supply section came by. After watching for a while, he approached John.

"You don't have any picture on your airplane," he observed. "I'm pretty good at those things if you can show me what you want."

We gathered around him and he mentioned that he was responsible for the nose art on several of the squadron planes. We had just not come to grips with the matter of artistic design, but it was now or never. You just don't find guys anywhere that can do good nose art. We kicked around many ideas but, finally, by consensus, we settled on the name "Wood's Chopper" because of John Wood's name.

Now, our artist friend began to suggest possible art forms. Gradually, the final design emerged. It would feature an upraised arm with a bloody ax over an executioner's block on which was a caricature of the Japanese Emperor. Beside the block was Hitler's severed head. Gory, but very symbolic of our resolve we thought. The Sergeant agreed to paint the design on both sides of the plane for twenty dollars. He whipped it out in about four hours while we worked on the wing.

There was one more distinction to be added--identification of our individual crew positions as seen from the outside. For an extra five dollars, our artist painted nicknames or other personalized items under the windows at our crew stations. Thus, under John's window was "Long John." Lubin's window featured "Pisonia," which sort of summed up his personal

Crew of the "Chopper".

philosophy. Ayers showed "Gumbo." I had two things painted on the window up front. The first was "Blondie" in honor of my girl. The second was a set of dice showing a "6" and a "4". I leave it to the dedicated crap shooters to decipher its meaning.

Now 42-7750 was ours for sure, and we never called her anything else but the "Chopper".

So, with our newly painted nose and our non-leaking tanks, we were ready to start upon our journey into the war at last. We left Bruning on the 23rd of November and rejoined our squadron at Topeka on that same day confident that our difficulties were over with the "Chopper". Alas, a further indignity struck our noble bird on 2 December. While she was sitting peacefully on the ramp awaiting our "go" command, a B-17 taxiing up the ramp hit the tail turret of the "Chopper" with its wing tip and knocked it off!

Topeka was a staging base where crews were briefed on the trip overseas and given their overseas combat gear. There was only a limited supply capability and spare tail turrets were not in stock. A requisition was placed through channels and we just sat there and waited. The rest of the group flew out on 10 December, and all of the group's hold baggage, including all of our records and our foot lockers of extra clothes that were going by boat, also left.

Finally, the tail turret came, was installed, and accepted. On the 21st of December, we, at last, departed Topeka for the final stop in the United States--Morrison Field at West Palm Beach, Florida. It was there that the seriousness of our situation, as far as the rest of our journey was concerned, became apparent: collectively, we were nearly broke. It was nearing the end of the month and, with no pay records, you just didn't get paid--at least not in the ZI, as any one who ever dealt with an Army Paymaster can tell you!

CHAPTER 3

We're On Our Way--But To Where?

How would you like to start out on a long journey with no idea where you will end up? We did.

As I mentioned, our final stop in the United States was at Morrison Field, West Palm Beach, Florida. We were all by ourselves, since the rest of the group was eleven days ahead of us and had long since departed for parts unknown. On the one hand, it was kind of relaxing to be free of the normal discipline of group operations--to pretty much do our own thing. On the other hand, I certainly felt a large amount of apprehension about my forthcoming role in this journey. I, who vividly remembered getting seriously lost flying up and down the San Joaquin Valley only a few months before--and who had logged little but dead-head time since--was expected to guide this airplane and the thirteen men aboard to some place guaranteed to be on the other side of some large body of water and in some other continent. I'm sure the same thoughts crossed John's mind--about me.

In case some have forgotten, in 1943 we were involved in a
World War. There were enough fronts that might require our
presence that where we were going was kept a big secret--even
from us. The Air Transport Command (ATC)--the guys who
delivered supplies, equipment and men to the war zones--had a
world-wide network of air bases leased from our friends or
captured from our enemies. Since they regularly flew most of
the same routes the bomber crews would be using to get to
their assigned bases, the ATC was given the task of shepherd-
ing those crews along the way. They did a good job although
many of us did our best to frustrate their orderly procedures.

The ATC network was much like the underground railway
in the days of slavery. When we poor, half-scared, migrating
"warriors" dropped in on their bases, the ATC people fed us,
housed us, refueled us, and briefed us for the next leg. Each
stopping place knew our next destination, but no one along the
way knew our final destination--not even the last base. On that
last leg, we operated under sealed orders which we opened just
before taking off.

The ATC, of course, had their own mission, and taking
care of bomber crews was not one of their favorite tasks. They
tried to do it with the least possible pain--to themselves. As a
result, they had some very strict rules governing the on-the-
ground behavior of the passing air crews. This created a
certain tendency on the part of the air crews to attempt to
subvert these prohibitions. After all, considering the fact that
we were on our way to combat, what could those ATC
"weanies" do to us that could be any more severe than having
our backsides exposed to hostile fire?

Our Christmas present from the ATC was a briefing for the

18

first leg of our journey--to Borinquin Field, Puerto Rico departing on 24 December, 1943--Christmas Eve. We arrived in a blinding rainstorm and vicious turbulence, and we had to circle awhile before things cleared up enough to land. They assigned us quarters--officers in one place, enlisted in another-- and left us alone, saying nothing about what was to happen next.

There was a very nice Officers' Club at Borinquin--up on a high bluff overlooking the ocean--a far cry from that miserable hovel at Bruning. The club had a marvelous dining room, with a package store attached, where one could buy all sorts of liquor at fantastically low prices. They even had a great PX with lots of things to buy close by. The problem was that the whole crew was virtually destitute. Our last pay was as of 31 October, and here it was nearly two months later. Some of our gunners were even worse off than we were. Although they were fed and bedded "on the house," they had nothing to spend at the enlisted clubs or the PX.

We called a crew meeting to discuss our situation. The future looked very bleak since we had no idea how long we would be in route nor how long before we ever got paid again. We were like orphans in the storm, having no squadron or group command structure to turn to. Now, only one day from the USA, we were in unknown territory with not a friendly face in sight.

Our salvation came about through the agile mind of our Co-Pilot, Lubin. Back at Topeka in preparation for our trip overseas, the Army had issued to each Co-Pilot a packet designed to help us should we crash along the way. The main ingredient, besides maps, water purifying pills, and messages

19

in several languages identifying us as Americans, was the magic passport--$500 in American currency. Now, this money was to be used only in an emergency if we were down in unknown territory and needed to buy our way to safety. The whole $500 was to be returned to the paymaster if we made if safely to our destination. "Silly"--as I used to call Lubin-- pointed out that emergencies came in all forms and what we were facing here on Christmas Eve was definitely a situation not planned for. Since we were operating on our own, John was the "commander most high," and all he had to do was say "yes." He did, and Silly doled out $20 to each of our thirteen people. That made Christmas much more merry!

Apparently, the ATC did not believe in working on Christmas because they gave us the day off. We loafed around, drank a lot of the free eggnog at the club, and filled up mostly on the lavish snacks laid out for club members. Since we were about the only "strangers" on the base that day, they generously let us pick at the goodies.

Warmed both by the hot Puerto Rican sun and the delicious eggnog, we five officers decided to try the gorgeous, clear blue waters rippling on the beach below the club. What a great thing to go swimming on Christmas Day! We climbed down the cliff to the beach and, since we had no suits, walked up the beach until we were out of sight of the club. We shed our clothes and splashed around in the ocean for about an hour. We dried off by walking around buck naked on the beach examining coconuts in their husks--something that most of us had never seen. Finally, we dressed and walked back down the beach towards the club. As we got nearer, we saw that there was a stairway leading up the cliff--we had missed it on the way down. At the foot of the stairs was a permanently implanted sign: "Beware of Barracuda"!

On 26 December, we were back in the air, our destination Atkinson Field in what was British Guiana. (The field was very close to where Jim Jones and hundreds of his followers committed mass suicide.) As we approached the field for landing, there below was a B-24 in the jungle just off the runway. It wasn't one of our group by its markings, but it sort of emphasized the point that flying can be hazardous to your health.

It was at Atkinson Field where I obtained the first foreign currency for my "shortsnorter" collection. Originally started by the pilots of the ATC, "shortsnorters" were quickly latched onto by the rest of we Air Corps flyers. It consisted of a strip of paper currencies stuck together with Scotch tape from all of the countries one landed in. At each base, you picked up a sample of the local currency and then had all of the guys around at the bar sign their names on the bill. Now, the next time you showed up at that base, you gathered more names on the bill--and usually a drink from the new signatories. Some of the guys who traveled a lot had "shortsnorters" eight and even ten feet long. I still have mine, but it's only about three feet long.

The ATC sent us on our way the very next day. We were not sorry. Atkinson was sort of the pits. It was then British territory and there were very few amenities. They briefed us and gave us maps for out next destination--Belem, Brazil. These flights were not long in duration--five or six hours--but they took us over some godawful-looking jungle. I kept my attention strictly on my maps being darn careful to establish a good track. Fortunately, the weather was good and we flew at reasonable altitudes, so the pilotage was not difficult.

21

In addition to the "fifty mission crush" hats, the ultimate fashion statement for the airmen who flew in foreign climes was the mosquito boot--often called the "Natal" boot because that's where you got the best ones. The Natal boots cost about $8 American and were the pride and joy of their owners who wore them constantly except when on combat missions. The temperature and the ever-present possibility of being shot down required more substantial footwear on a mission.

The Natal boot was so highly prized that demand frequently outran supply. I was incredibly lucky to obtain two pairs at Belem--the next best place to Natal for mosquito boots. When we landed in Africa, the first man aboard greeted us with fumigating chemicals and announced that he would pay $20 for every pair of Natal boots we had. No one was interested in a mere 240 percent profit!

From Belem, we flew on to a Navy base at Sao Luiz, Brazil. We were temporarily shunted to this out-of-the-way place because both of the main departure points for the transatlantic flights to Africa were loaded with B-24's and B-17's waiting to make the crossing. The pipeline was full, and we stayed three days at Sao Luiz.

Having done some serious shopping at Belem using an additional $10 each from the emergency kit, the whole bunch of us were close to destitution again. Lucky for us, we were in Navy rather than Army hands at this point. The Navy was notably nicer to its people and that spirit spilled over on us. We went over to see the Navy Finance Office and explained to the Chief in charge that we'd had no pay for two months and were all broke. He said that its being the end of the month he and his people were too busy to help us, but--if we'd do the

22

typing of the orders--he's give us a partial pay. What a splendid troop he was! We sat Lubin down at a spare typewriter,
and he pecked out a set of orders giving each of us half of the
two-months pay owed us.

Now that we were flush again, we put the money we owed
back in the emergency kit and still had a lot left. The Navy
was not as strict about leaving the base as the ATC people, so
we went into Sao Luiz to see what was happening and to
sample the local food. What we found was a gambling casino
with all the trimmings including a croupier who could count
chips flowing through his fingers faster than the eye could
follow. The Cruzeiro was then only worth a nickel, so we
played roulette with gay abandon--much to the excitement of
the natives. John and Silly, the more dedicated gamblers in
our group, would have stayed longer, but the rest of us wanted
to eat, so we left with most of our pay still with us. We departed Sao Luiz on the 30th for Fortalaza, Brazil--the jumping-
off point for our flight to Africa.

CHAPTER 4

On To Africa--And Back

As we approached the field at Fortaleza, we couldn't believe the vast number of airplanes sitting on the ramp. Our hearts sank. We figured that we, a crew by itself orphaned from its parent group, would be at the bottom of the priority list for overseas movement. Why were we in such a hurry to get to war? To tell the truth, we were lonesome for our buddies in the squadron. We missed seeing a friendly face in the mess line or at the bar in the club. The fact is, it took a long while for air crews to develop a close rapport with each other. In a squadron, there was often more of a bonding among crewmen of the same function. Thus, First Pilots tended to hang out together in a special fraternity. Even Co-Pilots were not admitted--they were viewed as apprentices. Navigators and Bombardiers similarly tended to flock together, and the enlisted Gunners followed the same pattern. When we were left alone among hosts of strangers, we did stick together as a crew, but that was by necessity and not by choice.

In any event, we settled into our temporary quarters in a

tent, marveled at the notion of eating fresh picked pineapple, and thought seriously about buying one of the little spider monkeys that native boys were hawking around the base. They were certainly appealing but very unlikely to survive the trip. And $20.00 was still important money to us in those days.

As was the case at every ATC stop, we were restricted to the base. But, as a special treat, the ATC laid on a bus trip--no stops--into Fortaleza on the 31st of December. It was interesting but not what most red-blooded American airmen had in mind when going to town--like going for a drive through the red-light district with Mom and Dad!

New Year's Eve was a very dull affair. We went to the club for a few drinks but the spirit just wasn't there. So, it was back to the tent and a book. As I look back now, with no radio, TV, newspapers, or other news media, we were sort of suspended in limbo at Fortaleza. As far as we were concerned, the rest of the world was blanked out and at a time when the most exciting part of our lives was happening.

New Year's Day 1944 started the same way--eat breakfast, drop by the PX, walk around a little, buy some more fresh pineapple, then, back to the sack for reading or a nap. We figured that this was our fate for the near future. It was not what Lubin had in mind though.

Syl Lubin was "different" from most of the guys we knew on the crew and in the squadron. In days long before the term "laid back" came into vogue, Silly fitted that term exactly. He went along with the military rules when they seemed to make sense to him. Otherwise, he just ignored them. He would do things so blatantly contrary to official policy that we all marveled at his audacity. To Silly, however, those things were no big deal. His attitude was: "So what can they do to me?" If you believe that way, you can have a lot of fun that the rest of us rule-followers missed out on.

Silly decided that he ought to explore Fortaleza by night. He tried to organize us into a party for the trip, but John, Fenton, and I, being more conservative, declined. We had a Co-Pilot from another squadron riding with us, however, and Silly talked him into going. We all figured that we'd be stuck at Fortaleza for a week or more so John didn't object to their sneaking off the base, figuring that they were big boys who could take care of themselves. They left about six P.M.

We settled down to an evening of reading and playing solitaire. You can imagine our surprise when, at about eight-thirty, a Sergeant from Base Operations drove up in a jeep and asked for Lieutenant Wood. When John responded, the Sergeant dropped a bombshell on us: "Lieutenant, get your Navigator and report to Base Ops at 2100 for your overseas briefing. You're going over tonight!"

Almost everyone today has made a long overseas flight. I imagine that at least one hundred planes a day make an ocean crossing. It's old hat now but, to a bunch of young kids in 1944, flying an airplane from Brazil, South America to Dakar, Africa over two thousand miles of ocean was indeed a big deal. The thing I couldn't believe was the casual way it came about. I gulped. This was the night I was really going to earn my pay as a Navigator.

John and I went to the briefing as ordered. There were a lot of crews represented--all strangers to us. A very hard-nosed, red-headed Major chewing on a cigar was in charge. It was obvious from his attitude that he was going to be very happy to see all of us on our way and out of his hair. We were briefed very thoroughly on all the necessary data including course, winds aloft, altitude, and time of take-off--2300 for us. The ATC was able to give us bomber crews excellent in-flight data since their own pilots were crossing and recrossing the same routes almost hourly. Take-off times were scheduled about every five minutes from ten P.M. until one A.M. the next morning. Thus, ATC was able to send off over thirty planes each night without their interfering with each other.

When the briefing was over, we returned to the tent to pack up our belongings and get them down to Operations. John elected not to mention that two of our crew were missing assuming that they would surely be back well before take-off.

As the clock moved forward to ten-thirty P.M. and no Lubin, it was obvious that confession was in order. In fifteen minutes, we were supposed to be starting our engines and taxiing out.

To say that the red-headed Major was not amused is the understatement of the year. He was furious. He chewed on John for not controlling his crew and threatened all sorts of dire consequences. He then called the MP commander and ordered him to get his people into town, grab Lubin and companion, and haul them back instantly. The MP's were dutifully dispatched and they quickly located the two "AWOLS." But, at this point, there was a communications breakdown.

The MP's asked Lubin, "Are you gentlemen scheduled to fly tonight?"

"Naw," responded Lubin. "We just got here. We won't be going for days."

Incredibly, the MP's let them go! Lubin and friend continued to sample the night life of Fortaleza until after midnight before sneaking back to base. When they found the tent empty, some guys in the next tent told them that we were all down at Base Ops. They appeared there, happy as larks and half "smashed," at one A.M.

The Major greeted them with a salvo of profanity. He chewed them out as succinctly as I've heard it done, ending with a warning to all of us:

"You bastards, get out to that fucking plane and go! I'm sending along a report to your commander and I hope he busts your asses! If I ever see you again, I'll have you court-martialed!"

In retrospect, the Major's wrath was understandable and justified. He was responsible for the movement of hundreds of crews to various combat theaters and every screw-up affected the operation of the pipeline. Perhaps we should have at least apologized. At that time, however, it was our fondest desire to get out of his sight quickly and forever. As soon as we reached the "Chopper", we fired her up and took off heading east. By this time, it was nearly two A.M.

Sometimes fate has a way of adding an extra "zinger" to an already sticky situation. It sure did this night. It was apparent to John as he climbed to our assigned altitude that the "Chopper" wasn't flying right. He was pulling more power than he should have had to get there and she was flying much more slowly than she should have at normal cruising manifold pressure. John didn't say anything to the rest of us. I guess he hoped that, as we lightened up from burning fuel, things would improve. After about two hours, I called Ayers, our Flight Engineer, to give me a reading on gas consumption. I was horrified to see how much we had burned and made a quick calculation on the flying time remaining to landfall. At the rate we were going, we'd be out of fuel four hundred miles from Africa!

I called John and told him the bad news. Now, John had to make a big decision. Should be believe his Navigator, who was relatively untested, or should he continue on for a while longer and check again? John was not at all happy about the consequences of turning back remembering the threats of the Major.

"Are you sure you're right, Currier?" he asked. "I hate like sin to go back."

"I'm sure," I responded. "We'll be over two hours short of Dakar, and I can't swim," I told him.

The rest of the crew were listening intently. Finally, he growled, "OK, but you better damned well be right, or I'll kick your ass all over that base!"

Whereupon he wheeled the "Chopper" around and I gave him a new course for Fortaleza. We landed at six-thirty A.M., a little more than four hours after we had left.

As we taxied to a hard stand, a weapons carrier approached us at breakneck speed. Who should be driving, but the red-

30

headed Major. Apparently, he had not yet gone to bed. As we killed the engines and got out, I thought he would die of a stroke when he saw us he was so mad. John tried to explain to him that something was wrong with the "Chopper" and that he had elected to turn back because we would have otherwise run out of gas. The Major didn't seem to believe us although I couldn't for the life of me figure how he could have suspected us of malingering after the send-off he had given us the night before.

Pointing a finger at John, the Major snarled, "You sons-of-bitches get over to the mess hall, eat, and get back here in thirty minutes! I'll fly this damn airplane, and if there's nothing wrong, it'll be your asses!"

He wheeled around, jumped into his vehicle, and sped away. We humped it for the mess hall, wolfed down some eggs, toast, and coffee and were back at the "Chopper" in the allotted time.

You may have noted that the date was now 2 January, and south of the Equator, this was mid-summer. As the sun rose, so did the temperature. We did our best to stay in the "Chopper's" shade, wishing that the Major would soon reappear. He never showed up until twelve-thirty P.M. We were pretty well cooked by then.

He was all business. "I'll take the left seat. Wood, you take the right." He glared at Lubin. "You stand behind." he growled.

The Major fired up the engines, taxied down the ramp, running the checklist as we went. He checked the four mags

31

on the fly, and, reaching the end of the runway, he pulled off all power on the right engines while shoving the left throttles to the wall. We spun around in a tight arc. As we swung through the axis of the runway, he pushed the right throttles full forward and we began to roll. The "Chopper" no more than broke ground when he yanked up the gear himself. John said afterwards that he thought we were gonners right then. The "Chopper" never faltered however. The Major climbed her out just above stall speed until we got to about four thousand feet. Then he proceeded to put her through a series of flight profiles.

After about an hour, the Major's attitude visibly improved. "The damned thing is loaded all wrong!" he said. Turning to Lubin he ordered, "Take all of the baggage from the rear racks and move it to the front racks. Get your playmate to help you," referring to the other Co-Pilot who had been out on the town with Lubin.

Now, the cat-walk in the bomb bay of a B-24 is narrow, and it is very difficult to move around in there. In the afternoon in the summer over Brazil, even at four thousand feet, it is sweltering hot. Lubin and the other Co-Pilot sweated like pigs while the Major directed them to move all baggage from the tail of the plane into the just-vacated rear baggage racks. At last he was satisfied that the plane was in proper balance and we landed.

As he left in his carrier, he gave John a parting order: "Be at Operations at 2200 tonight!"

We were there--all 13 of us.

We took off on schedule about eleven P.M. The flight was anticlimactic. The "Chopper" flew perfectly. The night was clear and the weather fine all the way. Three hundred miles out we picked up the Dakar beam and followed it in. We were only two degrees off. Not too shabby for my first real test. As a result, I gained a considerable amount of confidence from among the crew--especially from John. Oh, yes, we landed with four hundred gallons of fuel left on board, a very comfortable margin.

CHAPTER 5

We Close In On The War

To be greeted by a guy with a flit gun after your first flight across the Atlantic was somewhat deflating. I guess the Africans were afraid of catching something from Brazil--what that could be that they didn't already have, I couldn't imagine. In any event, after being fumigated, we disembarked from the "Chopper". It had been a long night--about twelve hours flying time. They took us to some tents and showed us where the mess hall was. We were hungry. The Army Air Corps did not believe in pampering its airmen. Except for the several candy bars we had bought on our own, we hadn't eaten for fifteen hours.

We stayed in Dakar for two days. Muller went over the "Chopper" with a fine-tooth comb and pronounced her OK. It was good to have Muller with us on this trip. He was a superb crew chief, but a white knuckle flyer. I can still see him hunkered down on the flight deck his ears cocked to the en-gines' tune and his eyes on the gas gauges. I figured that if it were humanly possible for a crew chief to keep us flying,

Muller could do it. And he had the greatest possible incentive to do it. His ass was on board too.

The next leg of our journey was North to Marrakech, Morocco. If ever a plane needed to be in good shape and a crew on the qui vive, this was the leg. Twelve hundred nautical miles from the jungles of West Africa over the virtually unexplored emptiness of the Sahara to the grim starkness of the Atlas Mountains which we could not fly over and had to penetrate--this was a real moment of truth. When we were briefed for the trip and given maps, I could hardly believe what I was hearing. There were only five visible checkpoints for reference in those twelve hundred miles! The maps covering a large portion of the Spanish Sahara were almost blank. Even the variance was not known over most of the way,and, of course, wind data was nil. In navigation school these factors were applied to all dead-reckoning problems, but here the briefer just gave us the "educated guess" on these values and told us to adjust it whenever we got a visual fix.

We started out and for the first hundred miles, we were right on the predicted course and hit the first checkpoint "close enough for government work." The next point, however, was a big black rock sticking up from the desert emptiness three hundred miles up the line. The briefer guaranteed that we would see it if we were anywhere near. It was supposed to be five miles East of our course. Waiting for that rock to appear was a tense period. I had a predicted time, but when that ran out--no rock. The problem was that we were looking in the wrong direction. The rock finally showed ten minutes late and about seven or eight miles to the West of course. Obviously, something was wrong with our wind data.

I made some course corrections and we pressed on to the next checkpoint--another four hundred miles beyond. You can't imagine the vast emptiness of this land! There was nothing--no roads, no villages, no rivers in this area. The ground was mostly flat, but one could see the hint of hills on the horizon--or maybe they were mirages. Our briefers were not optimistic about our chances if we went down here. They told us at all costs to stay with the plane and to be very very careful how we behaved if we were found by tribesmen. Some would help us and some would kill us for whatever we had. The odds were about fifty-fifty for either outcome.

We continued on, our eyes straining for the predicted checkpoints. Next was a basaltic escarpment a few miles to the West of course and, beyond that, a dim but well-used caravan trail crossing a deep wadi. By the Grace of God, we found them, made such course adjustments as needed, and droned on to the key checkpoint of the trip--the tiny desert town of Tindouf.

If you perceive the Sahara to be mostly brown, it was. But so was the town of Tindouf--a tiny island of humanity nestled in a vastness so great that it was nearly lost to the eye from any distance. Furthermore, it took on the color of the desert mud from which it was constructed, and brown on brown is not easy to spot. Apparently this had been a problem for earlier aerial passersby because--lo, and behold--just East of town was a big white circle with a "T" in the center. Now THAT's a checkpoint!

The next leg of the trip was only about sixty miles as I recall, but it was a most critical leg. It took us, at eight thousand feet, right up to the forbidding face of the Atlas Mountains that formed an impenetrable barrier to further Northern progress. The Atlas towered to fourteen thousand feet, and the trick was to negotiate them at eight thousand. Why? Because we carried no oxygen and humans don't function too well above twelve thousand feet without oxygen. How were we to get through the mountains? There was a pass used for centuries by camel caravans that wound its way through the jagged peaks to emerge in a lush oasis lined with date palms and guarded by the walled palace of the sultan.

Now, camels could take their time to thread their way through that rocky path, but airplanes must maintain flying speed. We flew straight for the mountains at one hundred fifty-five miles per hour. The closer we got, the more antsy John got. He could see that our time was running out and that either we bumped into the mountains or did a "three-sixty" and got out of there.

"Are you sure we're on course?" he kept asking me. I tried to reassure him that all was well. With such a precise checkpoint at Tindouf and such a short leg to fly, the chance of being off course and missing the pass was very low. But, the damned thing was impossible to see until you got right on top of it.

At almost the last possible moment, John shouted "I got it!" and he wheeled the "Chopper" into a rather tight left and began to let down. We twisted and turned through the rocky gorge, losing altitude all the way until we saw the greenness of the oasis. What a sight! The airfield was a few miles beyond. John "greased" her in. I, for one, was darned near wiped out. I devoutly hoped that I'd never see that route again. When we finally got to our base, we learned that Dave Council, Squadron Commander of the 716th Squadron and his crew, were lost trying to make it through the Atlas Mountains.

Who would ever guess that Africa could be freezing cold? Not we pilgrims from the West! But it was. We once again were ushered to a tent complex and issued some bedding. The bunks in the tent were nothing but a netting of ropes--no mattresses or other creature comforts. The blankets and sheets they gave us were supposed to make us comfy. They didn't. When the sun set at Marrakech, it turned unbelievably cold. The moisture content of the desert air was practically zero and, when the sun went down, there was nothing to hold the heat of the day.

The first night we shivered and shuddered all night long. When morning came and we were still held there, we got into our baggage to find some more appropriate clothing to wear. Since leaving the States, we'd been in summer time. We slept in our skivvies and had no problems. But now we needed more. I found what I thought was the perfect solution--my heated flying suit.

In the early days, bomber crew members riding in positions that required only a limited degree of mobility were issued heated flying suits which got their heat by plugging into the electrical system of the B-24. The suits were a handsome robin's egg blue color and were designed to be worn under a coverall-type flying suit. The suits even had heated feet and gloves. They were supposed to be worn only on missions, but they looked darned attractive as underwear in the frigid nights in North Africa. I, and several of the others, dug them out of the baggage racks and put them on. I didn't take mine off for nearly a month.

When we arrived at Marrakech, we still didn't know where we would end up. England and the Eighth Air Force was a good possibility, but so was the Thirteenth Air Force in the China-Burma-India Theater. You got there via the same route. Another possibility was Italy and the Fifteenth Air Force, although we knew very little about it. It had only recently been organized and begun operations in Italy. We awaited the next route briefing with great anticipation. Alas, it revealed nothing, except to direct us to Algiers and to a famous airfield--Maison Blanche.

The city of Algiers, which we were fortunate to have the chance to visit, was no desert town. It was a cosmopolitan city on the Mediterranean with wide avenues, attractive buildings and parks, and even hotels--most of which had been appropriated by the Army higher brass for their comfort and pleasure. Algiers was a French city without doubt, from the language of the people to the names of the streets and the menus in the restaurants. But, it was a city of contrasts. While many of the people dressed in conventional Western garb, the natives wore long, white, shapeless robes that covered them from neck to ankles. These robes looked for all the world like mattress covers we used on our bunks. Maybe they were. The Yanks had been here for over a year and were well dug in. I could visualize some very rich Supply Sergeants placing huge orders through channels for mattress covers.

We were lucky to find a room in a small "two-star" hotel on a side street for the one night they allowed us in town. We did, however, get a chance for a real hot shower and a comfortable bed with a spring mattress which seemed like heaven compared to our recent lodgings. It was the first decent time we'd had since leaving Puerto Rico--which seemed like ages ago even though it had been less than three weeks. Algiers picked us up tremendously.

The next leg of the trip was going to be very revealing as to our ultimate goal. We would either be setting a course North or we could forget England. They briefed us for Tunis, so that ruled out the Eighth Air Force for us. OK, we could live with that. The stories we'd heard about flying out of England against Fortress Europe hadn't been all that enticing. Now it was either the Fifteenth or the CBI.

We were at the top of Africa, close to the sea, and the amount of human activity was great. Lots of cities and towns and land features would make navigating a cinch. We headed out for Tunis with the sea to our left and the desert to the right. The habitable part of North Africa was a relatively narrow band along the Mediterranean. But, what a history had been lived out there from earliest days to the present!

As we moved across the North African landscape, we soon began to see signs of war recently fought. We noted heavily damaged towns and lots of abandoned, burned-out vehicles. From the air, it was also very easy to pick out the final results of the massive air battles which had taken place overhead. Crashed and burned aircraft were visible where they had fallen. What had happened to the gallant airmen on both sides who had flown them? One could not tell if they lay entombed in the wreckage or had lived to fight another day. It was a sobering thought.

When we approached Tunis and prepared to land, the carnage of war lay all around. The field was a one-directional runway of pierced steel planking. Surrounding the base was

41

the biggest aircraft junk pile we'd ever seen. We glimpsed the
carcasses of just about every plane that had fought there. Most
of them we'd only seen in pictures during our aircraft recognition classes in training. There were scores of German planes,
from giant JU-52's to Stukas and ME-109's. There were
Hurricanes and Spitfires. There were planes with French and
Italian markings--most of which looked woefully obsolete
beside our newer American types. But, there were some of
those there, too, in that aerial graveyard. It looked to us like
all of those planes had simply been bulldozed off the field to
keep it operational after bombing attacks. That, indeed, was
the case.

We stayed only one night at Tunis, but it was memorable.
Since we had arrived early in the afternoon, we had time to get
to our assigned quarters, get cleaned up, and change into our
"suntans." We got a bite to eat and were then ready to explore.
The closer we got to the war zone, the more relaxed were the
rules. We had no restrictions on going into town from
Marrakech on. It was simply a matter of finding some transportation. At Tunis, we found that there was a "six-by" truck
going in, so most of us hopped aboard--all but Syl Lubin and
Red Bauers, our ball gunner. They said they would follow
later. We got directions as to where to catch a bus back to the
base and its schedule. We were ready for some fun.

Tunis was another Frenchified North African city but with
significant Arab influences. Its architecture reflected the
mixture. Further, there were a lot more Arabs and a lot fewer
French, Americans, etc. We soon felt its mysterious presence.

We officers found what looked like a decent cafe and went
in for dinner. The other crewmen took off for further sightsee-

ing. After eating a quite good dinner, we ordered some of the local champagne. It was cheap enough, but it had a pinkish cast that made it look sort of rusty. A few bottles of this tasty wine combined with the warmish temperature of the very crowded room soon got to Fenton, who was not much of a drinker. We figured that we were reaching the end of our long trek and had not done at all badly flying the whole route by ourselves. Staggering to his feet, Fenton loudly proclaimed a toast to us assembled. We cheered and raised our glasses.

As Fenton's arm went up, it kept right on going. The liquid flew over his head and splashed all over the nicely pressed "pinks and greens" of an American Army full Colonel sitting at a table behind him! A very tense few moments ensued as the Colonel wiped himself off, saying awfully bad things about all flyers in general and about us in particular. Rear-echelon "ground-pounders" tended to react that way towards the Air Corps. We left. The eagles on his blouse seemed to indicate that that was the right thing to do.

After walking around a bit to clear our heads, we decided that we must see what a real-life Casbah looked like. Tunis had one, and a British soldier directed us to it with some very serious warnings about sticking together and staying away from side alleys. The Casbah was just a section of town inhabited by the native Arabs. In the daytime it teemed with all sorts of people shopping in the stalls and making lots of noise. At night, when we were there, it was quiet and sort of creepy, at least to me. I kept looking around for characters like Pepe le Moko and Peter Lorre. What we saw were men in their flowing robes silently sliding along the near-empty streets looking at us suspiciously. It suddenly occurred to me that, at least for the present, we represented the power structure. No one bothered us, and we left without incident. About midnight, we found the bus going back towards the base and boarded it. It had been an interesting night.

As usual, Silly did it a might differently. He and Red noticed a jeep parked near Base Headquarters with the key in it. They appropriated it and drove merrily off to town. There they abandoned the jeep as possibly a tad "warm," and proceeded to enjoy Tunis and its many pleasures. They covered the town like a blanket, meeting some other air crewmen and carousing until all hours. They were secure in the assurances of these other guys that they had a truck and would give them a ride back to base. When the night was over, they all piled into the truck and were deposited at the base. There was only one problem: Tunis had two air bases and their friends of the night were at the other one! Silly and Red limped into our base at six-thirty A.M., just in time to report for the briefing for our next stop on our road to war.

CHAPTER 6

It's Italy--But Where Is Grottaglie?

On 10 January, 1944, we finally found out where we were going to fight the war. At the briefing for our crew that morning, the Operations Officer handed John an envelope marked "Secret." John opened it, and there was the final destination--a place none of us had ever heard of called "Grottaglie." We eagerly poured over the maps they gave us. At last we found it--a small dot with an airfield symbol, on the heel of Italy about at the instep of the "boot." The city of Taranto, seven miles West, dominated the map in that area. It had been a major port since Roman days and was the site of a British strike earlier in this war that had sunk a good part of the Italian navy.

I laid out a course taking us from Tunis to this minor dot on the map. We would pass over Sicily--almost directly over the fabled Mt. Etna, then across the foot of Italy, the Gulf of Taranto, thence to our future home--a flight of four hundred-fifty miles or about three hours. We got off about nine A.M.

As soon as Lubin had yanked up the wheels and evened the throttles to a nice steady hum, he "squinched" down in his seat and promptly fell asleep. John shook his head in disapproval but set up the heading I gave him, and we headed for "home" at last.

It was a fine day and no big deal to keep track of our course. John, however, wanted to make damned sure that we were on course and not straying. We were now definitely in the war zone, and who could tell what might lay in wait for a single unarmed B-24, cruising along at a leisurely one hundred-fifty knots? He kept calling me and asking questions about what we were seeing down below, how were we doing on the course, and what about our ETA? I kept reassuring him that everything was fine.

It was--and still is--my belief that most Pilots never completely trust Navigators to bring them to their final destinations. In the States with many radio navigational aids available even in those days, Pilots would follow their Navigator's instructions, but with one ear cocked to what the various beams were telling them. Only when they were outside the U.S. and had nothing in the way of backup did they accept their Navigator as a full partner--reluctantly. Even though I had gotten us across better than seven thousand miles of unfamiliar land and water without outside help of any kind, I could sense that John was a bit uncomfortable pushing his throttles without being confidently sure of where he was.

John was really concerned when I finally told him that Grottaglie lay just ahead and he tried to call the tower for landing instructions on the frequency they gave him at Tunis and no one answered. He tried again and again. Nothing. We circled the base a couple of times at two-thousand feet. Nobody paid any attention. We could see B-24's on the field but couldn't recognize any of them by their markings.

Finally, John growled, "Currier, I'm going to land, and this better be Grottaglie, or your name is mud with me!"

The field was nothing to speak of--single-directional runway North and South, pierced steel planking surface, dirt taxiways, and grassy parking areas. Since he could not contact the tower, he never got any landing instructions. He chose his direction from the wind sock on the control tower, brought her in lightly, and rolled to a stop at the end of the runway waiting for a "follow me" jeep to show us where to park.

No one showed. It was like coming home for Christmas vacation after being away and no one even coming to the door! John slowly taxied the "Chopper" off the runway and down the taxiway towards one of the clusters of planes parked on the grass. He picked an empty spot and cut the engines.

We stayed in the plane for about five minutes, waiting for someone to show up or something to happen. Still no reaction from this apparently active base. No one, but no one, showed his face. Finally, we climbed out and looked around for signs of life. It was not a pretty sight. Off to our right were the skeletons of two massive hangars. Obviously, they had been destroyed. A couple of hundred yards to their left were several buildings, badly damaged, with gaping holes in their sides. Bomb damage for sure. One of the buildings--the least damaged--had some military vehicles parked beside it.

"Lubin!" John ordered, "Get your ass over to that building

47

and see if this is the right place! I can't believe no one saw us land! Find out what the hell the story is and get back here, pronto!"

Lubin ambled off in the direction of the buildings. The rest of us relaxed on the grass under the "Chopper's" wings. John, however, paced back and forth looking towards the buildings and watching Lubin sauntering towards them. We all looked around for friendly faces, but there were no faces, friendly or otherwise. This certainly didn't look like a fighting group to us.

Lubin was gone for nearly a half-hour, although it sure seemed longer to us. We kept watching for his lumbering form and didn't notice an Army truck approaching us from the rear. The truck pulled up and stopped and out stepped Lubin!

"This is the right place," Lubin confirmed. "They told us to unload our stuff and to go over to our squadron area--over that way." He motioned towards a grove of trees.

"Did you see anyone you know," John inquired, "and where did you get the truck?"

"Naw," Lubin responded. "That's Base Operations. All our squadron people are over in that area," he waved his arm.

"What about the truck?" John persisted.

"Oh, well," Lubin grinned, "it was just sitting there, so I borrowed it to get our stuff over to the squadron."

"Oh, God," John groaned, "OK. Let's get the stuff loaded

and get over to the squadron before they come after us. Lubin, you've got to quit screwing around now that we're back with the Group. As soon as we're unloaded, take the truck back."

We loaded our gear in the truck and all piled in. Lubin drove. We went across the grassy parking area, across a little bridge over a slowly flowing stream and followed a dusty road until we came to a series of pyramid tents--some in the trees and two or three much more smartly arranged in an open area. Now, we began to recognize friendly faces. We drove up to what were obviously the command tents. John got out, went in, and reported our arrival to Captain Nosker. At last, we were "home."

Almost immediately, Tom Chandler, a First Pilot and one of John's closest friends, appeared. He and most of the others had been at Grottaglie for about ten days, and they had been wondering what had happened to us. Chandler took us down a row of bedraggled tents and showed us an empty one sagging forlornly in its ropes under what turned out to be an olive tree.

"This one's empty." he announced. "Throw your stuff in here. You stay here tonight, and we'll move in with you tomorrow. By the way, where did you get hold of that truck?" he asked.

"Lubin just grabbed it over there at Base Ops when we got here," John replied. Turning to the rest of us he ordered, "Let's get this damn thing unloaded so Lubin can take it back!"

"Wait a minute, John," Chandler urged. "We're going to need transportation to move our gear and to scrounge stuff around here to fix up the tent. Let's just park the truck out behind the tent and leave it there. We'll just keep it until someone comes and gets it."

We did just that. We had the truck for our exclusive use for ten days. It was a godsend--more properly a "Lubin-send"--for us in getting our canvas home in order and our creature comforts attended to. When our willing steed finally disappeared, probably repossessed by it former custodian, we missed it but were able to live without it.

CHAPTER 7

We Set Up Housekeeping--Italian Style

We threw our gear into the tent--on the dirt floor because that was all that was inside. The tent had been hastily set up under an olive tree on reasonably flat ground. There it slumped waiting for us to make of it what we could. It was mid-afternoon by now, so we decided to look around the area and get familiar with our new home while trying to get the straight scoop from our friends who had been here for about ten days.

What we saw was living on a most minimum scale. Except for the tents, there were no buildings of any kind. Off to one side was a platform about six feet high with a tank on it. Running down from the tank and passing between two rows of limestone blocks was some copper tubing. Sitting on the blocks were some large kettles over which the squadron cooks were hovering. This was the mess hall--without the hall! Incredibly, these guys were attempting to feed over three hundred men with this rig. The fuel was gasoline running down the tubing by gravity and burning at holes punched in it.

The food was C-rations, and the cooks had to work almost continuously to get enough cooked or warmed to feed the multitudes. They were getting the evening meal ready in mid-afternoon.

"Where do we eat?" John asked Chandler.

"Right where you're standing," he grinned. "It's picnic-style. And we'd better get you over to the supply tent so you can draw mess kits."

We could hardly believe what we were hearing, but it all turned out to be true. That evening about four P.M., a line began to form, officers and enlisted intermixed, each with his mess kit and cup. The line moved slowly forward. Each man was doled out some stew-like glop, a piece of bread, and some canned fruit. Another helper filled our canteen cups with coffee--not very hot, but plenty strong. We moved away, found an empty spot on the ground, and sank down to pick at the food. After eating, we got in another line to empty out the leftovers and wash our mess kits.

It began to get dark, and it was definitely chilly. We went back to the tent, and it was as black as a tomb inside. We had no lights--not even a flashlight. We stumbled around trying to make some sort of bed out of the two blankets we had been issued. It was too cold to take off our clothes so we kept them on. The ground was hard and lumpy and none of us got much sleep. At this point, it seemed to us that the glamour of the Air Corps somehow had been left behind. "What happened?" we wondered. We soon learned the answer.

Few people are aware that the second greatest American

maritime disaster after Pearl Harbor occurred on the night of December 24, 1943 in Bari Harbor, Italy. The harbor was crowded with ships--all loaded with supplies, equipment, and munitions--much of it destined for the rapid buildup of the Fifteenth Air Force in Italy. German intelligence was extremely good. When it was observed that a big bottleneck had developed in unloading ships, the German Air Force struck on Christmas Eve with a devastating air raid. Virtually every ship in the harbor was sunk or heavily damaged. Among those ships was the one carrying all of the base support cargo for the 449th Bomb Group. And that had happened just two weeks before we got there! No wonder things were disorganized at Grottaglie!

The next morning, after a breakfast of powdered eggs and Spam, Tom Chandler, Bob Winters, Pete Ihrie, and Dave Livingston dumped their gear into our tent and we all set off in our borrowed truck, with Lubin driving, to scrounge up the amenities for our canvas home. It was a great help to have Chandler's crew with us because they knew the territory and were well informed about where to go and what to do.

"Head for that low building over beside Base Operations," Chandler directed. "That's Engineering, and that's where they put all of the anti-icing tanks they've taken off the airplanes. They don't use them in combat--they burn if hit. We'll need one for our stove," he explained.

Next stop was an aircraft "graveyard" where the wreckage of a number of German airplanes were piled. We looked for some tubing from their fuel systems and a petcock. We'd borrowed tools from the boys in Engineering and were able to salvage about twenty feet of usable tubing and a shut-off valve.

53

We threw them into the truck and headed for the bomb dump.

Our first view of the ammunition dump at Grottaglie left us amazed at the amount of raw destructive power lying around in careless abandon. At that point in time, our ordnance people simply took over the German dump and stored our American bombs in the same place. Later, the ordnance experts removed and exploded the German munitions. Now, however, box after box of German machine gun ammo, twenty millimeter cannon shells, and bombs of various sizes and shapes lay scattered around the area. To one side was the American ordnance-- mostly five-hundred and one- thousand pound bombs and boxes of fifty caliber shells for our machine guns. The munitions were not our objective, but their containers were.

American bombs came separate from their stabilizing fins. The fins were encased in pressed steel "cages" to protect them from damage in shipping. The parts of the cages were bolted together. When Ordnance was ready to load bombs, they removed the cages and screwed the fins onto the bombs. The cages were then taken back to the dump for salvage. If one took the cages and reassembled them in a different way, they made great chairs for the tent. We loaded up enough for eight chairs, although we found that that was too many for our cramped quarters.

The Germans packed certain of their bombs in wooden boxes about four-feet long. The wood was pine, and the boards were about six inches wide and three quarters of an inch thick--excellent for building a table for the tent. We secured enough for that purpose and then headed for the two big hangars that stood like gaunt skeletons near Base Operations. The hangars were all that remained of the Italian dirigible operations for which they were justly famous before the war. (Does anyone remember the "Roma" and the "Norge"?) The hangars had been bombed out in the American attacks the previous fall. We drove up and parked. We needed a floor for our tent, and the small cement floor tiles loosened by the bombing were just the ticket. After loading what we needed, we headed back to our area. Now commenced our home improvement program.

The first thing we did was to reset the stakes, straighten the center pole, and tighten up the ropes of our tent. This not only made it look better, it gave us some much needed extra space. Next, we tiled the floor with the tiles we had removed from the dirigible hangars. This proved to be a mistake. We hadn't thought about the stove and its fuel lines which we wanted under the flooring. We propped the anti-icer tank securely in the lowest crotch of the olive tree beside the tent and ran the tubing down the side of the tree and under the tent side. We buried the line in the dirt of the floor and re-laid the tile over it. Now, we were ready for a stove.

Our tent mates knew just what to do about that. There were some Italians who had already been hired by the squadron to do certain unpleasant tasks around the area. The natives were desperately poor. The Germans, in retreat, had scarfed up everything that moved or was edible leaving their former hosts nothing. The people were glad for anything they could beg from us, and to have a paying job was a miracle to them. One of the Italians had sheet metal-working skills. For a carton of American cigarettes--like gold in those days--and the materials to work with, he would build us a stove and chimney. We got him a five gallon oil can and the metal liners from several fifty caliber ammo boxes. From these meager materials he constructed a very serviceable stove which kept us cozy warm throughout the cold and rainy winter and spring.

Safety experts of today would react in horror if they had seen our stove and the way we all slept peacefully around it. The stove was simplicity itself: a five-gallon closed container with holes punched about two inches above the bottom and filled up to that point with crushed limestone was the burn chamber. The copper tubing we got from the wrecked airplanes entered the stove from the rear about six inches above the limestone. The shut-off valve to control the fuel flow was just outside the stove body. The fuel dripped from the end of the tubing onto the limestone, where it burned smartly. And the fuel? It was good old one-hundred octane aviation fuel-- the same kind that drove the American Air Corps to its heights of fame!

When we got to Grottaglie the engineers had not had time to lay in the fuel pipelines that later brought the gas needed for our operations from the port of Taranto. So, all of the gas used came in containers made famous by the Germans in the Africa campaign--the Jerry-can. There were thousands of them lying around in the middle of the field, full of gas. All we had to do was drive out there in our truck, pick up several to last for a week, and bring them back to the tent. Each day, one of us kept the anti-icer tank filled.

In the early days, our stove had a certain design problem relating to the rate of flow of fuel. The fuel rate had to be precisely tuned so that the amount burned would equal the amount dripped. If the gas flowed in too fast, it would not all burn and would gradually fill up the limestone and flow out of the holes, down the legs of its stand, and then out into the cracks in the floor tiles. Suddenly, and very disconcertingly, the floor would erupt in flames and we would all run outside and throw sand back in to put out the fire. The fix for that problem was a second shut-off valve outside, near the tank, to control the flow. With both valves properly set, we had no further problems and slept soundly, without worry, at night.

With the floor laid, the stove in place, the chairs assembled, and the table built, things looked better for us. Tom and Pete went into town and bought two oil lamps and extra chimneys for light. The first few days we slept on the floor. Then the base engineers came up with four double-decker bunk frames welded from angle iron salvaged from the hangars. We shoved them deep into the sides of the tent.

Back over to the salvage yard we went. There we laid hands on some German camouflage netting and some of the miles of telephone wire they had abandoned in their hasty flight. The netting, wrapped around the bunk frames and secured with the wire, made a very serviceable bunk. We were definitely in business when Supply got in some foot lockers so we could store our gear.

From time to time, we made certain refinements to the tent but, basically, we were ready to hold an "at home" for the rest of our friends and we did.

CHAPTER 8

Combat! That's What We Came For

If you were to ask a woman what emotions she felt on that special day when she lost her virginity, she would probably respond: "anticipation and apprehension, exhilaration and relief." I think most of us felt the same way when, on the night of 12 January, 1944, John came back from a meeting with Captain Nosker and told us we would be going on a mission in the morning.

As I look back to those days after having spent a career in the Air Force of today, it seems incredible that we would be flying a combat mission with so little training or experience. There we were just two days in Italy. We hadn't flown so much as a single hour in high-altitude formation since we had left Bruning in November. Bob Fenton, our Bombardier, had dropped exactly ten practice bombs in two sticks with the Sperry bombsight with which our plane was equipped. Our gunners had never fired a single shot at any target from the "Chopper." We didn't even know whether the turrets worked. Obviously, the powers that be were very anxious to get some-

59

thing going on the underbelly of Europe.

The Fifteenth Air Force had barely been organized when two groups of B-24's and a group of B-17's were moved up from Africa to Italy. The B-24 groups were the 376th and 98th Bomb Groups which had made the famous, but disastrous, low-level raid on Ploesti in August 1943. They flew B-24-D model airplanes painted a pinkish color to blend with the desert sands of North Africa. We called them the "Pink Elephants". These groups began operations in the late fall of 1943 but, with no long-range fighter escort, their attempts to raid up into Austria and Germany resulted in such heavy losses as to cause them to cease operations until they were reinforced.

The 449th and 450th Bomb Groups were the reinforcements. We were the first B-24 groups to come to Italy directly from the States. We, together with the 376th and 98th, made up the 47th Wing--the first complete wing in the theater. A lot more wings were to come--sixteen in all, but there was no wasting time in getting us operational.

The next morning, 13 January 1944, our squadron operations officer, Rex Thompkins, came poking into our tent about seven A.M., focusing his flashlight on John.

"Let's go, John. Briefing's in forty-five minutes. The weather looks good. No problems", he said cheerily.

We didn't need Rex's wake-up call. We were all awake just lying in our bunks thinking our own thoughts. "What was it going to be like?" "Would we do it right?"

We all sprang out of bed and put on our flying suits and the ever-present leather A-2 jackets. It was cold and damp outside. We had very little to say to each other except grunts as we headed for the mess area. Chandler and his crew were not going on this mission so they stayed snug in their blankets pretending to be asleep. The powdered eggs were about half warm and the bread was cold and untoasted. Only the coffee seemed worth consuming. The sky was brightening and we could see that it was going to be a good day. We washed our mess kits and headed back to the tent to drop them off and to pick up our briefing note pads. Then we trudged off across the field to Base Ops.

Later on, when we'd had much more experience, we'd have known one thing: when they let you lie abed until seven A.M., it's going to be a short mission. For some reason never revealed to us, the Fifteenth Air Force liked to bomb at high noon and frequently on Sunday. Maybe it was to give the Germans indigestion on their lunch break. More probably, it had something to do with the sun angle for target recognition.

As we entered the briefing room, we saw a large map of most of Europe on the wall. This was our first of many visits to this room and our first view of that fateful map with its piece of red yarn-like material laying like a gash across its face. We quickly learned that this piece of red went from Grottaglie to where ever our target for that mission was situated. Today, the line was fairly short--Northwest about three-hundred miles to Perugia, Italy.

While waiting for the briefing to begin, we glanced nervously around the room to see who else of our friends were there. There were a lot of unfamiliar faces. Except when flying missions, squadron people stuck pretty much to themselves. It may sound strange but, in all the time I was in the 449th Group, I never set foot on the "turf" of the other three squadrons. Most of us in the 718th didn't even know where they were billeted.

A Group effort consisted of thirty-six planes with a couple of spares should an airplane have engine trouble before take-off. Usually the group drew as evenly as possible from the four squadrons, so each one contributed nine crews. At the briefing, Pilots and Co-Pilots of each crew sat with other Pilots. The Pilots had a very keen interest in who was leading the box in which they would be flying and who were their wing men. Pilots, over time, developed a lot of information about the flying abilities of other Pilots in the group. Under conditions of high-altitude formation flying in combat, it was good to know those all around you.

Navigators and Bombardiers of each crew sat with each other. They worked closely together as a team in the air and shared a lot of information in the briefing. The rest of the crew were not required to attend the briefing.

The briefing officer, Major Bill Tope, approached the platform with pointer in hand, and the room fell silent. The briefing began. It was roughly divided into four segments. The first part was the general mission briefing. This covered the target, a German airfield; the initial point from which we would start the bombing run (the IP); the route to and from the target; and the enemy defenses we might encounter on the way and over the target. That day light, inaccurate flak was pre-dicted, and we novices brightened up at this report. Later on, we learned that how much was "light" flak and how "inaccu-rate" was this flak was definitely a judgement call and not a promise!

The second part of the briefing was the weather both en route and over the target. It was our experience in most of our missions that this was right on the mark. It was then. American reconnaissance pilots had flown the route, examined the target, and reported back the data just a few hours before. It was a good thing. In those days, we had no radar or other navigational aids, other than the eyeball, to find our targets and later to find our home base on the return flight if the weather turned bad.

Next was the Navigator's briefing dealing with courses to fly in and out; IP information and how to recognize it; winds aloft; and places to avoid en route, if possible. At this time, the briefing officer would give all of us a time "hack"and we would set our watches.

Finally, the Bombardiers would get their briefing. It covered target details; aiming point; bomb loading; fuze settings; bombing altitude; bomb ballistics; and intervalometer setting for the spacing of the bombs on the target. Much of this information had to be preset into the bombsight. We Navigators studied the target pictures closely with the Bombardiers. It was a joint effort to pick out the target and the aiming point before the Bombardier could go to work.

The briefing concluded with the Group Chaplain, Father McNamara, praying for us and we doing the same, silently, for ourselves. We headed back for our squadron area to pick up our flying gear.

We walked slowly out to the "Chopper". Muller was

standing beside her as he always was. John and he discussed the condition of the plane which was all OK. John and Lubin did a walk around. Ayers, the Flight Engineer, was busy doing his pre-flight check--tanks full of fuel, caps wired down, bomb racks loaded OK, no oil leaks, etc. The rest of us, having nothing to do at this point, sprawled out on the grass under the wing. We talked nervously about mostly nothing at all. We gave the rest of the crew the basic briefing details--target, predicted flak, the P-38's who would escort us. We tried to make it seem routine, but I don't think we fooled anyone. Just about then, a carry-all drove up to our site and dropped off our chutes, "Mae West" life vests, flak vests, and helmets.

About nine A.M., a green flare arched gracefully up from the control tower. The mission was on! We climbed into the "Chopper". John and Lubin ran down the checklist and fired up the engines. We taxied part way out, waiting for the airplane that was to take off just before us to get in the line of planes on the taxi way. The group took off at about thirty-second intervals--when the plane in front was about two-thirds down the runway.

We followed the routine we had practiced at Bruning for forming up the group. Our leader, Colonel Alkire, slowly circled the field at about three-thousand feet. The object was to get two sections of eighteen ships each formed up. These sections each had three elements of six ships, and the whole thirty-six had to be properly nested together for protection and to make a good bombing pattern. This was no simple matter, and with so little practice, it took a long while to get each Pilot into his assigned position. We could almost hear the "Old Man" fuming as we went round and round.

64

When every one was loosely positioned as planned, Alkire took off flying about North to cross over the Italian coast at Vieste, the "spur." We stayed out over the water, skirting the coast to avoid flying over the German lines which were anchored on the East at Pescara. We turned back inland below Tolentino and headed for our target. Perugia is just off the Tiber River in an area of marshes. The surrounding hills and the marshes were covered with snow. Landmarks were obscured, and the Lead Navigator couldn't find the target. I looked desperately for something I could recognize. Nothing.

Suddenly, we saw the lead ship opening his bomb bays. Fenton did the same, as did most of the others. He couldn't recognize a thing, but he put his finger on the toggle switch and waited. When the bombs began to fall from the lead ship, he toggled ours. Gravity took them to earth-- where, no one knows. We saw about four bursts of flak off to our left and way below. I don't know why the Germans bothered. We certainly didn't do them any harm.

Alkire headed us for home in deep disgust. We didn't envy him. He had to report this debacle to the Wing Commander. It would not be a pleasant session. We landed back at the base about two P.M. and were debriefed. There was nothing to report, and we were all pretty disgusted. We went back to our squadron area. Our friends who had stayed home wanted all the details. We had nothing to say.

And so ended our first combat mission. The score--no runs, no hits, and plenty of errors--about what one should expect from our level of experience. Well, we would go again and again until we got it right. We did, finally, but not before we had paid a heavy price.

CHAPTER 9

We Begin To Pay The Price

The day after the debacle at Perugia, we were in the air again for a short two-hour mission to Mostar, Yugoslavia. Our target was the town itself, because it was the headquarters of the German army in Yugoslavia. Once again, our inexperience and lack of training resulted in a failed mission. This time, however, it produced a tragedy--our first combat loss--and we did it to ourselves.

Formation bombing requires that the Group be properly lined up and tightly bunched for the run into the target. For these reasons, an initial point (IP) is selected as the beginning point for the target run. The formation is supposed to be brought to the IP, which is sufficiently distant from the target itself, so that the group may wheel into position for the run in. From that point on, the formation will fly straight and level down the azimuth to the target. The target run must be long enough to give the Bombardiers a good chance to spot the target and to synchronize their bombsights on it. Target runs from fifteen to twenty miles long were most commonly used.

Mostar, Yugoslavia

68

And, believe me, for those other than the Pilot and the Bombardier who were very busy, the time to target seemed like an eternity as the enemy did their best to knock us down.

At Mostar, due to a navigation error, Alkire took us way inside the IP--within flak range of the guns defending the town. He tried to line up the formation but no use. We were almost over the target and still turning as we passed over the bomb-release point. The Germans were having fun shooting at us, but not hitting any one because of our circling over them. Then, Alkire did the one thing that we learned must not EVER be done--he took us around again. This time we did turn over the IP but, by now, the formation was in total shambles.

As I mentioned, in those days, the group flew in two eighteen ship sections. Each section had three boxes of six ships each. These boxes were each vertically separated by about one-hundred feet so that there was a high box to the right, a level box in the middle, and a low box to the left. The second section was similarly organized, and we were flying in the middle level box of that section. As we went down the bomb run a second time, all of the Pilots were desperately trying to close up the formation and line up for the target run. Just as we reached the bomb-release point, the high box of six ships drifted right over our box, and a Bombardier from the 716th released his stick of five-hundred pound bombs. I was looking out my window at the time and saw the first bomb strike our wing man right at the top turret. There was a tremendous explosion, and that plane carrying Pickard's crew disintegrated into little flaming pieces. It happened in an instant, and it was hard to believe that these guys who trained with us and who lived in the next tent to us were gone.

Pickard's plane was about one hundred twenty-five feet from us, and the concussion was stunning. John did a fantastic job of wrestling the "Chopper" back into position and avoiding a collision with the planes around us. That we were not hit by flying debris or shrapnel from the bomb was amazing.

The plane that dropped the bomb was not so fortunate. The bomb bay doors were open, and the whole blast came up into it. Isgrigg, the Pilot, temporarily lost control; the plane slid out of formation, narrowly missing his wing men and heading for earth. Isgrigg punched the bailout button and some of the crew in the back bailed out. At that point, he began to get a measure of control over his airplane, but it was badly crippled and far below and behind the formation. Isgrigg ordered his Co-Pilot to go back and assess the damage. The Co-Pilot took one look at the broken, twisted hydraulic lines and bailed out himself. Isgrigg and his Engineer somehow nursed that airplane back across the Adriatic to Grottaglie and crash-landed it on the field. For that feat of airmanship, he got the Distinguished Flying Cross.

At the debriefing, several of us who had witnessed the destruction of Pickard's ship were all in agreement. No one could have survived. Forty-one years later I learned that, in fact, two guys did get out--the Tail Gunner, Robert Hansen, and a photographer taking pictures that day. The reason they survived, according to a letter Hansen sent me, was that the whole tail section of the B-24 broke off at the waist windows and it floated down like a falling leaf giving those two who were back there plenty of time for an easy bailout. They were captured as soon as they hit the ground and, along with the Co-Pilot and several crew members of Isgrigg's ship, spent the rest of the war in prison camp.

Alkire must have felt that he was snake-bit after these last two missions. Nevertheless, the group kept on flying, and Alkire kept on leading the formations. He swore that he would fly every mission the group flew despite direct orders from the Wing Commander to rotate with his Deputy and the Group Operations Officer, Major Bill Tope. And he did. Of course, that kind of behavior does not lead to job longevity. Alkire lasted three weeks and nineteen missions before they finally shot him down on 31 January, 1944 at Aviano, Italy.

Our crew did not fly another mission until 24 January, although we tried. The supercharger on our number four engine kept acting up, and we had to abort two missions. Muller worked like a dog trying to fix the thing. I can still see him in the cold twilight of the Italian winter standing on a fifty-gallon drum, working on that supercharger. In the end, he replaced it and we had no more problems with the engines on the "Chopper". She was one helluva airplane, and she fought a gallant war once she got over her early growing pains.

Now, in the 1980's, the targets we were attacking then with our heavy, high-altitude bomber formations--airfields, rail yards, troop concentrations--would be called tactical targets. Now, we would hit them with low-flying fighter bombers of our Tactical Air Command--A-10's, F-111's, F-15-E's, etc. Then, the tactical forces were not available in the numbers needed, nor did they have the range, so the heavy bombers did the job.

One class of targets that had to be taken out--if we were to get up into Germany, Austria, and the Balkans and survive-- was the German fighter fields in northern Italy, and Southern Austria. In the winter of 1943-44, the only fighter forces we had to protect the bomber formations were short-range P-38's. They could only escort us up to the top of the Adriatic. Then, we were on our own. The Germans counted on this fact and, most of the time, they made us pay heavily in blood.

In northern Italy, up near the Yugoslav border, were two German airfields at Udine and Aviano. They were about thirty miles apart. On 30 January, we carried fragmentation bombs to Udine hoping to destroy any airplanes caught on the ground and the facilities that supported them. We were flying in the "Purple Heart Section" that day in the low box in the second of the two eighteen-ship sections. It was so called because planes in that low rear box had no covering fire protection from other bombers behind them and thus were a favorite target for enemy fighters coming in on a rear pass. In fact, the whole box was made up of our squadron crews.

On the way up the Adriatic, one crew had engine problems and had to abort. That left five.

We were next. One of the guns in our tail turret jammed when Smitty test fired it and he could not clear the jam. Then, to make the cheese more binding, Red Bauer reported that the reticle sight on his ball turret would not turn on so he had no sight. Now, the "Purple Heart Section" is no place to be when you have no rear protection. John pulled out of formation and climbed up into the middle-level box of the section, and we became the seventh ship--not very neat, but a damned sight safer.

We proceeded on to the target at Udine, and everything went well up to the point of bomb drop. The frag bombs were little--about thirty pounds each. They were bound together in

72

clusters of three with steel bands that immediately came free when the bombs fell from the bomb bay. To our horror, we flew directly into a whole rain of steel bands from the ships in front of us. They bounced off the "Chopper's" wings and props, and scared us half to death.

Everyone dropped on target, and it looked like a good raid. But, once again, inexperience got us into deep trouble. It takes a great deal of flying skill for a group or section leader to rally off the target after "bombs away." The trick is to remember the guys behind you. The leader must stay straight and level until the whole group has dropped and then make a controlled, descending turn away from the target. He must be sure that he does not turn too tightly or let his speed increase, or his wing men on the inside will be stalling out while the wing men on the outside are struggling to keep up. The second section leader did it exactly wrong. His turn was too tight and his speed too high. The four airplanes in the rear of the second section found themselves flung way out from the rest of the formation--sitting ducks for the wave of German fighters who appeared out of nowhere and swarmed all over them.

This was the enemy "first team", we found out later--an elite ME-109 squadron recently transferred from the Western Front--to counteract our build-up of heavy bombers in the Fifteenth Air Force. Their prop spinners were painted yellow, and they were known by some as the "Yellow-nosed Devils". In about a minute, three of the B-24's out of the four in that last box were knocked down. Only Harper's crew survived by getting back under the protection of the rest of the group.

People have asked me in the past what combat flying was really like. It's hard to describe because it's so damned personal. A man's war is what he sees in his immediate vicinity. Unlike the movies where the photographer is outside the picture looking in, we were inside and our views were very limited. I saw just one of the B-24's all ablaze and going down. It didn't register in my mind at all what that fiery sight really meant in human terms. It was truly like watching a movie scene. I felt nothing. Then, I became heavily engaged in our own survival--calling out positions of ME-109's coming in on direct attacks on our formation. It was only later that I learned from some of the gunners who were watching, that two B-24's were knocked down by cannon fire and that the other was, in fact, rammed by a 109. Apparently, the 109 Pilot, on a head-on pass, had been hit by the B-24's guns and, out of control, had pulled up into the B-24's belly. Of the thirty men aboard those three B-24's, five survived. One was Dave Livingston--Bombardier of Chandler's crew who were our best friends and tent mates. Of course, at the time, we did not know this.

The next few minutes were wild indeed. The Germans turned their attention to the rest of us having done with the easy pickings. They came in from all directions. We were all on the intercom--no radio discipline at all. This was our first encounter with fighters. Everything before had been flak and, up until Udine, not very threatening. All of our usable guns on the "Chopper" were firing, and what a jolting noise It was! The 109's pressed their attack quite closely for a time and then appeared to back off some. We were heading South, and I guess they were beginning to worry about running into our P-38 escorts who were waiting for us to get within their operational range. Finally, the P-38's appeared and the Germans left. We flew home--back the way we had come, sadder and much wiser about what combat in the air really meant. When

74

we got down below oxygen level, I crawled up to the flight deck from my station in the nose. The floor was covered four inches deep with fifty caliber shell casings from Ayer's top turret. They took several boxes of casings from the waist, too.

When we landed that Sunday afternoon after Udine, it was a sad sight to see our tent with the four empty bunks and all of the personal things of Tom, Bob, Pete, and Dave lying around just as they had left them. We didn't know the proper procedure to deal with their things, so we just left them alone that night.

By now, we had a sort of combined mess hall and club built of unpainted green wood by the engineers. We all walked over there to eat and to talk over the mission and find out more about what happened. Chandler's crew, Wheeler's crew, and Kendall's crew were missing. Another First Pilot, Fletcher Porter, had flown on the mission as Co-Pilot for Kendall, and he was gone, too. No one knew who might have bailed out of which airplane, although it was known that some chutes were seen. We were a very subdued crowd that night.

The next day, our Exec told John to get together the things of the missing guys in our tent. We went through their personal belongings to make sure there was nothing objectionable going to be sent home. We packed their personal stuff in their footlockers keeping out candy and cigarettes and the government-issued equipment. We kept what we wanted of that and turned the rest in to supply. The foot-lockers were locked, and the Supply Sergeant loaded them in his jeep for transport over to Group and, ultimately, for the long journey home to their next of kin.

After we were done, we tended to the empty bunks, stripping their blankets and rolling them up. That was it--very final

75

and complete. We knew that some day there would be some new guys coming in, but we were not ready to think about that then.

Aviano was still left. The following day, 31 January, the Group went back up there and did the same thing to the field at Aviano. The flak was very bad, but the fighters were much fewer in number. We later learned why from Intelligence. These two raids had destroyed two-hundred German fighters in the air and on the ground! Now THAT was why we were there.

Alkire and his wing man were hit over the target at Aviano. Most of the crewmen successfully bailed out and were captured. We knew this from the reports of the returning crews. The Germans later confirmed it in one of their propaganda broadcasts. They gloated over the fact that they had shot down a Group Commander. They never mentioned the two-hundred aircraft we had destroyed.

Alkire was a tough Commander and a real "salty dog" of the old school. Almost everyone in our Group was either afraid of his wrath descending on them or, having experienced it, hated his guts. As I mentioned, he went on every raid the group flew--nineteen in all- until he was shot down. He lasted just three weeks.

It was common talk around the Group that the Germans would have a real problem dealing with Alkire because he was too mean to keep. We speculated that, any day, a JU-88 might appear overhead and the Germans would bail him out over us. It never happened, and he spent the rest of the war in Stalag I. After the war, he was promoted to Brigadier General and

served in various capacities. He passed away in the late "60's-
-one of the few "old bold" pilots from the early days who died
in bed.

CHAPTER 10

There Is Life After Death

It was a damned good thing that all days in a combat unit were not like that Sunday at Udine. In those early days of January, we were all that were available to fly against the Germans, so we flew a lot. Our crew and the "Chopper" only completed five missions in January, although we started out on two more and aborted. The group, however, flew nineteen missions in January, and that was a lot of action. Even though some of the missions were dismal failures, they all were learning experiences. Later on, when more groups arrived in Italy, we settled down to a more normal routine of one mission for each crew every three or four days.

When we were not flying, we had little to do, and we made the most of it. Unlike the spit and polish airmen of today, we were a raunchy lot. We were almost always attired in the combat crewman's uniform when it was cold--flying suit, A-2 jacket, mosquito boots, and baseball cap. When the weather warmed up, we shed whatever was too hot and lounged around the squadron area in tee-shirts and under-shorts. When we went to town, we hung a forty-five automatic in a shoulder holster under our armpit. This was considered proper in a war zone until a few shootings occurred when guys got drunk. The MP's then ruled out the forty-fives.

We shaved maybe once a week. We had no hot water at the base, so we just heated some in a can over our stove. It was a pain in the neck to bother to shave at all. The only reason most of us did it from time to time was that one's face itched like crazy when wearing an oxygen mask.

Bathing was not a frequent function, although most of us would have welcomed more opportunities. We never had such facilities at Grottaglie and had to go to Taranto for bathing.

The one thing we did not get involved with was girls. We might as well have been living in a monastery. There simply were none around the area. I saw one good-looking girl in Grottaglie. Things were not much better in Taranto: most of the girls we saw on the streets were pretty ugly. There were a few presentable ones in some of the restaurants, but they were always with some Italian and seemed to look upon us with disdain. We wondered whether the Germans had carted off all of the good-looking ones when they pulled out. Probably, the few presentable ones left were Fascist remnants of Mussolini's crowd.

Bill Nosker, our Squadron Commander, a clean-cut Nordic blonde, was an athlete--an All-American football player at Ohio State. Nosker was a Frank Merriwell type and an incipient "iron-ass." It plagued him to see his troops in such disarray. And we were a sad-looking bunch. As I pointed out, we were mostly unshaven and unwashed. We drank as much wine as we could find since we had no place to go for hard liquor. We smoked, gambled, slept late in the morning, and took afternoon naps when not flying; hustled food out of the mess hall for late-night snacks in our tents; and searched for any form of entertainment we could find. Like kids, we caught little salamanders with grass nooses. Some of the guys went over to the ammo dump, got some German shells, and took the powder from them--either to make rockets or to blow things up.

Bill Nosker made Major in the spring of '44 and, almost coincidental with his promotion, decided to introduce PT back into our lives. PT--or physical training--was never a popular item with us, even as cadets. We thought we were done with it as officers and, surely, as combat crewmen. Nosker prevailed, but on the basis of his rank alone. Every afternoon he got everyone out on the grass near the squadron area and led us in an hour of calisthenics. Oh, the moans and groans as unused muscles complained bitterly! Guys were having to be boosted into their airplanes to go on a mission. Fortunately for us, Nosker's order for PT was all-inclusive. It even embraced Dr. Bill Conway, our Flight Surgeon. After about a week and a half of this collective torture, Bill put a stop to it in the name of medical prudence. He hurt just as much as we did!

Nosker was not to be outdone, however. His next move was to organize teams of baseball players among us. He was most enthusiastic about this, and he got some tentative re- sponse from a few of the more athletic types. But, Bill Nosker was too competitive for his own good. While attempting to run out a long hit, he tripped and fell on a stone jutting up a ways out of the base path. He hit it hard enough to rupture his spleen, and he was hauled away to the hospital where he remained for weeks. That ended the PT movement in the 718th.

Nosker returned to the squadron in June looking thin and worn. In July, he was sent by the Wing to fly lead in the 376th Bomb Group for the mid-July D-Day landings in Southern France. He and all aboard were killed when the aircraft crashed on takeoff. There is a dormitory named in his honor at Ohio State.

The loss of Chandler's crew created a problem for us. We had left Topeka, Kansas, on the 21st of December and, because of the uncertainty of how long we were going to be at any of the stops along the way, we didn't dare to send out any laundry. By the time we got to Grottaglie on the 10th of January, we were reduced to re-wearing underwear and socks we had stuffed in our mattress-cover bags almost two months before. We desperately needed some clean clothes, but it wasn't until the 20th of January that we had time to do anything about laundry. Chandler's crew, having had about ten days start on us, had been into Grottaglie and had located a woman who would do laundry.

Our first visit to the town was very interesting to us. We looked at the shops--practically empty--and watched the people moving sort of listlessly around. When the Germans were driven out, they took with them every movable cart, wagon, or other vehicle, and every bit of food and wine in town. They left the people nothing, and the people were close to starving. We watched the women standing in long lines with their pieces of cloth, waiting for their small allotment of flour--I guess from the Americans. We looked at the ancient houses with their bundles of twigs and small branches on the roof. This was the fuel they cooked with.

At last, we got to the woman's house, picked up the clean laundry and left ours. We paid little attention as to how we had gotten to her house and didn't even know her name.

We never got a chance to get back our laundry before the 30th. Finally, on the 2nd of February, we hitched a ride into town and tried to find our laundress. We looked for hours for something familiar, but we really couldn't recognize a thing.

It was late in the afternoon, and we had despaired of ever finding our stuff when we ran into an Army MP who was on patrol in the town and could speak Italian. What a break! He started asking the natives if they knew anyone who did laundry for the Americans. Not a few of them were very sullen and pretended that they knew nothing. I was surprised. I thought everyone loved us Americans! Not so then, nor now.

Finally, we got a hit, and the person led us to the house we were looking for. The woman was absolutely delighted to see us. She had been very fearful that someone might accuse her of stealing our clothes. We thanked her and paid her and gave her a good tip. Then, we took some notes as to the name and number of the street and the name of the woman herself. We had learned that things are very uncertain in war time.

Another problem even more pressing than laundry was baths. Our last one had been at Tunis on the 10th. By the 20th, we were all pretty gamey. Once again, our buddies had the answer. We hitched a ride from Group Headquarters to Taranto, about seven miles away. There was a bunch of us all going for the same reason--a bath. The truck drove up to a large, dark building which turned out to be a public bath. We paid twenty-five lire for the privilege--bring your own soap, towels, etc. It sure was nice, and for the rest of our stay in

Italy that's where we got ourselves clean.

Haircuts and shaves were easily come by in Taranto. There were all kinds of barbershops along the streets. Haircuts cost fifteen lire. What surprised us was to see little kids about twelve years old shaving people with straight razors. It cost twelve lire--twelve cents--for a shave. As poor as the people were in those days, many of the Italian men went to the barber for their shave every day. It was sort of a male ritual, I guess.

With a bath and a shave we felt much better. Our next stop was an Officers' Club run by the British but open to all officers of any service. It was in an old building and was not a very lively place. You could get a sandwich and a roll and a cup of tea. The only liquors were wines and cognac, and the most popular drink was a half-and-half vermouth and cognac. It almost makes me sick to remember it!

Taranto, as well as our base and the surrounding country-side, were in the British sector for administrative purposes. The Brits controlled the area, and there was a wide assortment of Empire troops including Sikh's, Ghurka's, and Australians. Two things really amazed us American newcomers to Taranto. The first was seeing those turbanned Sikhs--very fierce-look-ing cookies. The second was seeing sizable numbers of blacks on the streets--and they were speaking Italian like it was their native tongue, hand motions and all! Having never seen any blacks before except American Negroes, it was a real cultural shock for us to hear them. How naive and isolated we were! We never remembered that Italy had an African empire for years before the war.

CHAPTER 11

We Meet Some Of Our Allies

Syl Lubin became quite curious about our British friends on the other side of our airfield. We used to see them take off and land--some flying night missions in Beaufighters and Mosquitos, some flying the old Wellington "Wimpys" on supply drops to the Partisans, and some flying Hurricane fighters in close support of the ground forces along the front. One day, he sauntered over to their operations shack about a mile around the perimeter of the field from our area. He was welcomed warmly by some of the troops standing around outside the place because he was one of the few Americans ever to visit them. They turned out to be Royal Engineers. They commiserated with him about the long walk, and one of the engineers had a bright idea. He sold Lubin a British motor-cycle standing outside operations for $25.00. Lubin was a bit uncertain about the transaction, but the Brits assured him that it was OK. They said that the motorcycle was one abandoned on the battlefield in North Africa and that it belonged to them for salvaging it rather than to the British Government.

Lubin was delighted with his purchase and he came riding up to the tent and spun the cycle around with a flourish. We were all envious of his new-found mobility but dubious about the validity of the purchase at that fantastic price. No so, John. His mouth literally watered at the possibility of getting one for himself.

"Let's go over and see if they've got any more, Silly," he urged.

Silly was agreeable. "Hop on the back, and we'll ride over," he said.

John sat on the rear fender, holding his long legs up, and away they went.

Of course, the Brits had another one--a bigger and better one that, according to them, had likewise been liberated and was available for sale, but at $50.00. John whipped out his $50.00, handed it to the Engineer, and he and Lubin took off. I'm sure those British Engineers were counting their money with glee and searching around their base for any more unattended motorcycles expecting to do a land office business in hot bikes. It might have happened except for two things.

Like all pilots, John was a dyed-in-the-wool "hot-rodder." He loved to ride that cycle. He was always trying to get Lubin to race with him. They would go round and round the squadron area much to the distress of Captain Nosker. Finally, Nosker had enough and laid down the law: "No more riding in the squadron area!" This didn't bother John. He was already tired of just going around the area and wanted a long straightaway for more speed. He and Silly took their bikes out on the road to Taranto and were having a high old time when a British lorry on the "wrong" side of the road chased John off over an embankment, totaling the motorcycle and banging him up with numerous bumps and bruises. He was stiff and sore for days and should have gone on sick call, but he didn't want Nosker to find out. John went on a mission during that time, but he let Lubin do most of the flying.

The second thing that put an end to the motorcycle business happened when Lubin decided to ride into Taranto on his bike to take a bath. He parked it outside the bathhouse, went in, and had a nice long shower. When he came out, his bike was nowhere in sight and a British MP was standing nearby.

"Did you see anyone take a motorcycle parked here?" Lubin asked.

The MP gave Silly a level stare. "Right on, Matey," he responded. "That's ours."

"Hold on!" Lubin protested. "That's my motorcycle! I bought it from a British Engineer at Grottaglie. He told me that he picked it up on the battlefield in North Africa and it didn't belong to anybody!"

"Lieutenant," the MP stated flatly, "that's the property of the British Government, and the British have recovered it!"

And that was that. Silly finally found a truck going back to the base and glumly boarded it. He decided that it wouldn't pay to protest to the British engineers.

The Brits were never thrilled with our presence near them.

They fully subscribed to that enduring refrain: "The Yanks are overpaid, oversexed and over here!" Although we did meet some real fine Empire troops--especially Australians--the Brits, themselves, were not above trading on our naivete as they did in the case of John and Silly. But one of them really reached the height of "consmanship" with a not too bright Co-Pilot in our squadron. He sold our guy, for $200.00 cash, a fully flyable Italian fighter plane that had been abandoned at Grottaglie when the Germans left. Our man taxied the thing around the perimeter to our area. He was actually planning to fly an enemy airplane over our air base! Nosker damned near lost his icy composure on that one. He called Group Maintenance, and they hauled the plane away to some undisclosed location.

Our crew had flown seven missions--barely beginning our tour--when, out of the blue, came the news: "You're going to rest camp!" I can't for the life of me figure out why, but Silly and I were selected among the first officers in the squadron to go. It was to be a three-day interlude. When we returned, John and Fenton would go.

No one knew where this rest camp was. We'd heard that the B-25 units on the other side of Italy went to Capri for rest and recreation. That sounded great Alas, our "rest camp" turned out to be an old hotel far down on the heel of the Italian boot at a town called San Caesaria a Mare. Incredible as it may seem, we were sharing this garden spot with Yugoslav Partisans who were ferried over to Italy to rest and refit from their efforts against German troops in Yugoslavia.

The rest camp was exactly that--all there was to do was rest and eat. It was the only time in my entire stay in Italy that I ever got any pasta. We also had some good Italian dishes such as Veal Scallopine and Chicken Cacciatore made by the hotel chef who must have headed up the kitchen in the days before the war.

It was interesting to have the opportunity to meet and talk with the Partisan guerillas. Talk about tough--one kid had been bayonetted right through both cheeks by a German soldier when he was seven years old. Now he was nearly ten and had already killed seven Germans in response. A sixteen year old girl--a shy, pretty little thing--was a sniper with sixteen Germans to her credit. And they didn't even count Italians whom they scorned as fighters. They liked us, and we found ways to communicate since many of them spoke some English. We gave them cigarettes which they dearly loved--even the ten year old. They would accept them if offered, but they were too proud to ask for them. I thought they were nice people.

The three days went quickly, and we were trucked back to the base. John and Fenton and the rest of our gunners then went for three days. While they were gone, Lubin and I flew a mission to Poggibonci, but in two different planes. This was one of the few times we all didn't fly together as a crew. Silly went with another plane, and he almost was shot down. The flak was very heavy and accurate. Silly's plane came home with over two-hundred holes in her. I went in the "Chopper", and we only took eight hits. Strangely, the "Chopper" never did seem to draw flak like some of the other planes and, for that, I was very grateful.

Silly and I were glad when John and Fenton returned from rest camp. We never felt right flying with someone else. Their trip to rest camp, however, was marred by a senseless tragedy.

Smitty, our tail gunner, had an infected mouth that had been bothering him since Tunis. It finally got so bad that he went to the flight surgeon who promptly put him in the hospital for a couple of weeks. In his place, we were assigned a gunner from another crew. He was a heavy drinker and some thought he was a malingerer since he missed some missions. Nonetheless, he went to rest camp with the rest of our gunners. The last night there, he got drunk and fell out of a second-story window landing squarely across an iron railing on the ground floor patio. It killed him. We made the long trip up to the American cemetery at Bari to bury him. It was not the last time we made that trip.

CHAPTER 12

The Big Week

Anyone who flew in bombers in February, 1944 will never forget the week of February 22 to 28, 1944. We all knew it as "The Big Week" and it surely was. It was a maximum effort to disrupt German fighter production to insure air superiority for the Invasion later in June. Up until that time, we in the Fifteenth had been working only in Italy and Yugoslavia, for two reasons. First, there were only a few of us--the buildup of the Fifteenth had hardly begun. Secondly, we had no long-range fighter escort--only the short-range versions of the P-38. What happened to the 376th and the 98th in November and December of '43 and to us at Udine and Aviano in January made it very clear that German fighters ruled the skies over southern Germany and Austria. Invading their skies would be very, very costly.

The week began on the 22nd, and the target was an aircraft manufacturing complex at Regensburg, Germany. The target was well protected by several airfields and a lot of flak positions. From our base at Grotagglie, it was six-hundred miles to the target up over northern Yugoslavia, through Austria, and into Germany, past Munich, with all kinds of enemy fighter bases along the way. And, once we reached the top of the Adriatic, we were on our own. That was as far as the escorting P-38's could go.

When we were briefed for the mission, we were more than a little upset to find that our Group was carrying fire bombs--the old kind, each weighing sixty-eight pounds and filled with jellied gasoline. These little beauties didn't have a spinner on the fuse but only a flat striker which had an arming wire through its shaft. As soon as the bombs were released and the wire pulled out, they were armed and ready to blow if the striker were hit. The Ordnance Officer made a big case for not dropping these bombs through the bomb bay doors--a frequent mistake by excited bombardiers on several of our earlier missions. He said he doubted that they were heavy enough to knock out the doors, as a five-hundred pounder would do. Thinking of those things bouncing around loose and armed in the bomb bay really got our attention.

Everything was peaceful as we crossed the Yugoslavia shore east of Trieste and turned Northwest. It was not long before we picked up some enemy fighters, and they harassed us for nearly an hour-and-a-half. We kept on going and, at last, after what seemed an eternity, we approached Regensburg. The day was mostly cloudy, and the target was partly obscured. As we began our bomb run, we saw an amazing sight--scores of B-17's from the Eighth Air Force in England a couple of thousand feet below us and coming off the target. This coordinated attack by the Eighth and the Fifteenth was one of the most effective raids of the air war.

German fighters never flew into their own flak. They would circle outside the flak area and wait for cripples coming off the target. And there were plenty of them because the flak was the most intense that we had ever seen up until then. This was a very important target for the Germans, and they did their best to stop us. Let me say at this point that, regardless of the opposition, no bomber force in the Fifteenth was ever stopped before dropping its bombs. The Germans could scare the hell out of us and disrupt our bombing accuracy, but they could never turn a formation back. They didn't at Regensburg either, even though we were still novices. Regensburg was the tenth mission for our crew.

There were several groups ahead of us going over the target. They carried the five-hundred pounders to make the kindling, and we were to set it on fire with our fire bombs. When our turn came, we went down the target run and, as far as I could see, everyone's bomb bays were open. Not everyone did impressive bombing, however. I watched one plane salvo, that is, dump its bombs after it was hit by flak. They fell out like a big bunch of sticks tumbling and hitting together in the air. When they hit, they exploded with a big flash and lots of black smoke. I could just imagine what a hit by flak or a twenty millimeter shell would have done to one of our planes while those bombs were still in the bomb bay.

That was the last time we ever carried the old-style fire bombs. Shortly thereafter, thermite bombs were introduced-- bundles of hexagonal, aluminum "sticks" fastened together with bands that flew apart after the bomb was safely on its way and scattered these thermite sticks over a wide area. They made a very hot fire and were almost impossible to put out.

The real air battle began in earnest as we rallied off the target. Our formations were still pretty ragged compared to our later raids, and we had several planes that had been hit and couldn't keep up. Our group had only put up twenty-five planes for this raid instead of the usual thirty-six because of attrition up to that point and maintenance problems. The fighters, knowing that they had a free hand, worked us over with deadly efficiency for over an hour. They shot down six from our group that day and heavily damaged several others.

An event took place on this first Regensburg raid that probably saved a lot of us in the 449th. It's not a pretty story, but it's true. Our "running mates" in the 47th Wing were the 450th Group stationed at Manduria, Italy, sixteen miles south of our base at Grottaglie. They came overseas at the same time we did and, we in the 449th, generally flew side by side or in train in front or behind them on a mission. The planes of the 450th had their two big rudders painted white, and they were nick-named the "Cottontails."

At Regensburg, one of their planes was hit over the target, lost an engine, and fell back. German fighters swarmed in for the kill. The pilot, seeing little chance of survival, let down his wheels--a recognized sign of surrender. All but two of the ME-109's pulled away. The two left closed in and took up positions flying in formation with the crippled B-24 as they guided it towards their base. Seeing that the battle had moved away from them and that the two ME-109's were like sitting ducks, the pilot ordered his gunners to shoot them down and they did. Unfortunately for our side, at least one of the German pilots was able to bail out and tell his story. That night, we were listening to Axis Sally on the radio in the mess hall. She recounted the story of this action and then said, "Our pilots have vowed to destroy you people in those planes with the white tails. They promise that they will wipe you out for this terrible act!"

From that point on, it was obvious to us in the 449th that the Germans meant exactly what they said. They would come charging in on us but, upon seeing planes of the 450th nearby, would leave us to attack them. At first, the men of the 450th tried to brazen it out. "Hell no! We'll keep our cottontails!" they bragged. But things got so bad that they changed their minds and painted their tails green like the rest of the planes. No matter. A day later, Axis Sally was back on the air telling everyone that the Germans knew of the change and were not fooled. The situation became so bad that they completely changed the tail markings of all of the planes in the whole 47th Wing, but, again, to little avail. The Germans had a remarkable intelligence network. Within days, Axis Sally was again describing the new markings of the 450th.

Was that single act of folly by that 450th Pilot at Regensburg costly? In the six months our crew was flying combat, the 449th lost sixty-three B-24's. In that same time, the 450th, flying next to us, lost one hundred-ten bombers.

CHAPTER 13

The "Big Week" Continues

The next day, the 23rd of February, we went up to Steyr, Austria, about a hundred miles west of Vienna. The same situation as at Regensburg occurred. The Germans were really fighting back with a vengeance. They gave us fits all the way up for one of the longest hours of my life. The Germans were using all kinds of aircraft to work us over. There were ME-109's, FW-190's, ME-110's and rocket-firing ME-210's.

It was on this raid that I suddenly and shockingly realized that war could be personally deadly. I was looking out my side window to see what was happening when I noticed a whole row of little gray puffs dancing just beyond the leading edge of our left wing. My first reaction was to wonder what they were. Suddenly, I knew. Those were exploding twenty millimeter cannon shells from some awfully close ME-109! Three feet closer in, and we'd have been full of very nasty holes and probably on fire.

A few minutes later, I was attempting to spot enemy fighters, which seemed to be attacking from all directions. The nose of a B-24-H was never made for sightseeing in any form. We had two small side windows sort of low so you could only glimpse a few things--mostly our wing men--to the side. The nose turret offered the Nose Gunner an excellent view from the front but, when he was in the turret, I couldn't see anything because his body blocked the view. The only place where I could look out and see anything was the astrodome--a small Plexiglas bubble above me. Around and below the rim of the bubble was a heavy steel flange about three inches wide. It was the mounting ring for a Navigator's astro-compass-a gadget most of us never used except in training.

Now, if you poked your head up in the astrodome, you had a three-hundred-sixty degree view of the world above our airplane and that's where the enemy fighters were. There was only one problem. We were issued regular Army tin helmets, just like the infantry troops wore, along with flak jackets to protect us. We wore the helmet perched on top of our regular leather helmet when we were under attack. The "pot" sat on top of our earphones and, when I would try to look out, the pot hit the top of the astrodome and wouldn't let my eyes get above its rim, effectively eliminating my view entirely. So, I took the pot off.

I was doing great work calling out the fighters to the gunners when there was a loud "clang" right beside my left ear. I ducked, pulling my head in like a turtle.

Just then, John shouted over the radio, "Eephus, put your god-damned helmet on!" (Eephus was a nickname I picked up over there.)

I did just that, and that was the end of my observing.

When we got down below the oxygen level, John called, "Come up here a minute, Eephus! I want to show you something."

I crawled down the passage and climbed up on the flight deck. John pointed towards the astrodome. A bullet had gone in and hit the flange right beside my ear making a five-inch gash in the "Chopper's" skin. I wore my "pot" from that point on and left the looking to others.

On the way up, we shot down our first enemy plane--an ME-110. Ayers in the top turret and Smitty in the tail got him. It is an exultant thing in an air battle, where everyone seems to be shooting at you, to see an enemy go down. The ME-110 seemed to stop dead in its tracks and then headed straight down in a vertical dive until it disappeared. It was not on fire and no one bailed out, so I assume the pilot was killed or badly wounded. You don't think about a man being in that airplane and headed for eternity until much later.

As usual, the fighters left us alone to face the intense flak of the Steyr defenses. We could see them all over the sky just waiting. At that point the flak seemed a lot less awesome. We were a long way from home and in awfully hostile circumstances.

As we rallied off the target, our gunners erupted in shouts. They had spotted a lot more fighters diving down from the North. These new planes came screaming in, and then they flipped up on their sides in a flashing turn so that we could all see them. They were our little friends, the P-38's so uniquely shaped with their twin booms. They flipped up so that we would know them. They then turned on the Germans with a fury and, within minutes, the skies were empty of any opposition. Suddenly, they too were gone, leaving us alone but safe for the journey home.

How did those P-38's, known by both sides to have only about a three-hundred miles radius when flying escort, get to Steyr and surprise the Germans so completely? Their commander, Colonel Hershell Green, devised a most clever plan. Normally, the P-38's would pick up the bomber formations going North near their bases at Foggia and then fly close-in support up to the head of the Adriatic. That was the limit of their range. They then would turn back and we would be on our own. We knew this, and the Germans knew it, too, so they would wait until they had us all to themselves.

On this Steyr mission, Colonel Green held his fighters on the ground until we were well on our way to Steyr. They then took off and flew directly to the target. By so doing, they saved a lot of gas that they normally burned crisscrossing over and around our slow-flying bombers. They had darned little gas left for the trip home, and some of them went into an airstrip on the Yugoslav island of Vis. A few ditched in the Adriatic. We heard that this heroic action earned a citation for the P-38 group and a Distinguished Service Medal for Colonel Green. If so, it was well deserved.

We only lost one plane that day, but it was from our own squadron. The Pilot's name was Wingfield, and his Flight Engineer was a boy named Fred Nelson, who was a friend of mine from my home town of Brockton, Massachusetts. They were hit on the way up to Steyr over the Alps in Austria. If

100

one has not flown over the Alps in winter, you could have no idea what a cold, desolate place it was if you had to bail out. Five of the crew in the back of the airplane did bailout and were picked up very much the worse for wear by the Germans. The guys up front, including Fred, were killed apparently when the plane was hit, and they went down with her somewhere in a deep, snowy ravine. Their bodies were not found until June, 1950, six years later.

The 24th of February was a "stand-down" day, but on the 25th we were briefed for Regensburg again. We took off in clear weather, but the ground in and around southern Germany was obscured by undercast, and there were also some higher clouds--a really rotten day for visual bombing. We were pretty well spread out in loose formation, and as we got up into Austria the group split into two parts because of weather. Fifteen planes went on to Regensburg, and the second section of twelve, including the "Chopper", turned off to our alternative, Graz, Austria.

The planes that went on to Regensburg were heavily attacked by fighters after coming off the target. One plane, the "Sophisticated Lady" flown by Gil Bradley of the 716th, lost two engines and was dropping way back. Bradley's best friend, Ed Drinan, against all orders, dropped back to help. In a running battle over the Alps into Yugoslavia, the crew of the "Sophisticated Lady" shot down fifteen German fighters before she finally went down herself. Drinan's crew also shot down several more fighters and circled the area where their buddies had bailed out until it was clear that the downed crew were not being attacked.

Bradley and his crew escaped detection and made their way

South until they encountered some of Tito's Partisans who cared for them and eventually helped them to return to Italy. Every man on that crew received the Distinguished Flying Cross for that action, and Bradley and one of his gunners got well-deserved Silver Stars. That raid cost the 449th three more planes--a total of ten shot down and four more so badly damaged in the three days that they had to be salvaged.

By this time, we were seriously depleted of flyable aircraft, and we badly needed some replacement crews, too. The problem was that the buildup of forces into new groups in the Fifteenth Air Force was absorbing all of the planes and crews available, and there just weren't any replacements. It was April before the 449th was able to build back to strength--just in time for the really serious bombing campaigns in the Balkans.

The "Big Week" did a lot of damage to the German fighter production, and they also lost a lot of fighters in air combat with our bombers. But hitting aircraft factories did not stop the German air forces. In fact, the Germans were producing and deploying more aircraft by the fall and winter of '44 than they had been before our February raids. It took the analysts a long time to figure out the simple answer to the stopping of any modern mechanized fighting force--oil.

One final note about the "Big Week." It was policy in the Eighth Air Force in 1944 that a tour in bombers was thirty-five missions. In the Fifteenth, however, the tour was fifty missions. After Regensburg, where both of us were over the same target, it was obvious that there was a certain inequity in tour length. The matter was resolved by giving us double credit for missions up into Austria and Germany and for the biggies in the Balkans--Budapest, Bucharest, and, above all, Ploesti. Thus, I ended up with thirty-eight sorties to get my fifty missions.

CHAPTER 14

March--We're Under The Weather

The weather, which was worsening during the "Big Week", really turned sour at the end of February and through most of March. No more missions were flown in February, and only six were completed by the group in March. Our crew only flew two missions in March, although we were briefed and got all ready for at least eight. Unlike the Eighth Air Force, we had no beacons or beams to use to assemble in bad weather or to find our field when we returned. Also, it wasn't until early May that we received the "Mickey" radar equipment which was available only in the lead airplane of the group and which was very limited in its usefulness. So, if the weather were bad or predicted to be bad--either over our field when taking off or returning or over the target--we stayed home.

It rained for days, and the field got soft and bumpy. On one of the two missions we flew, my chest pack parachute fell out of the nose wheel-well on takeoff due to the bumpiness of the field. I had been used to storing it in the passageway leading up to the nose and then taking it with me when I crawled up there. Fortunately, the mission was a "milk run" to an oil storage depot in Yugoslavia. Best of all, I didn't miss my parachute until we had bombed and were part way home. At least my time for worry was greatly reduced! From that time on, I kept my chute right with me all the time.

One of the tower people saw my chute fall out on takeoff, and they sent a guy out to pick it up. He did--by the red handle, spilling the silk all over the muddy runway. The parachute riggers were not happy.

When you don't have anything serious to do, you try to kill time doing just about anything. It was easy to get "cabin fever" living in a relatively small tent with seven other guys. We played a lot of cards--cribbage, pinochile, hearts, and the like. At night, the big gamblers met at the mess hall and played far into the night. We had a radio hooked up in the mess hall, and each night we listened to our favorite disk jockey--Axis Sally and her side kick, George. Why not! She played the best music, and her messages to us were so heavy-handed as propaganda that we laughed over them. One thing that did kind of get to us was her frequent messages to the 450th. She would welcome new crews by name and tell all about them. She would tell them that they would soon be guests of the Germans. I'm sure she made a lot of those guys pretty shaky. It would have worried me to have had her mention my name in that context!

The rainy afternoons in March really depressed us. I used to go up to the mess hall to try to find someone new to talk to. We had no drinking rules in the squadron, mainly because there wasn't anything worthwhile to drink. In all my time in Italy, I had one bottle of a weird concoction called "Anzio

106

Beer." It was beer, but awful. The only whiskey I ever had were the two ounces of Old Granddad that Bill Conway, our Flight Surgeon, doled out to us after a mission. We had to stand there in front of him and down it on the spot.

Gin was only slightly more available because the Brits had a supply of that. We made friends with an Aussie pilot who traded us gin for American cigarettes.

Our tiny bar in the mess hall had only a few exotic liqueurs, which came from heaven knows where, but outside the mess hall was a large fifty-five gallon wooden barrel filled with a deep purplish wine. We called it "Purple Death" and we paid the club a nickel a tumbler--a very large tumbler. In the absence of anything better, I used to drink a glass or so of the stuff in the afternoon. It made me sleepy, and I'd go back to the tent and take a nap.

One afternoon, I was there by myself nursing a tumbler and watching the Italian POW's clean up the mess hall. When Italy quit the war, these guys quit also and were paroled. They lived in barracks in town and came out daily to work. One of them, the leader, kept looking at me, so I smiled at him. He smiled back and then, pointing at my tumbler of wine, shook his head and said, "No buono".

Now, I didn't speak any Italian, but I understood his meaning very clearly. I nodded. "No bono".

He broke into a torrent of Italian, but I held up my hand to stop him.

"No comprendo," I protested. "You speak English?" I asked.

"No, No." He looked sad. He tried several other languages, but they were nothing to me until finally he said. "Tu parle Francais?"

That made a connection--not the greatest, but one that could be used and improved. My French was the product of three years of it in high school and, rusty as I was, I felt that we could converse. What a splendid feeling to finally make a communications breakthrough!

Luigi, I learned, was his name. He came from northern Italy, not far from Venice. He had a wife and several children there. He had been an interpreter for an Italian Alpine division and had deserted when Italy left the war. He made his way South until he met the British army and surrendered. Luigi could speak seven languages, but English wasn't one of them. He hated and despised the Germans as, according to him, did most of the Italian troops.

As my French came back, we spoke of many things. The first day, however, he wanted to be sure I didn't drink any more of that "purple death."

He said, "Tomorrow, I'll bring you in some wine from our own mess". True to his word, the next afternoon he had his army canteen filled with a light russet-colored wine. It was probably a cheap table wine, but infinitely better than the rotgut I'd been drinking. I gave Luigi two packs of American cigarettes as a gift in exchange, and he was overwhelmed. American cigarettes were worth almost as much as gold for trading on the black market. That night, I finished his canteen of wine--about a liter--and gave it back to him the next afternoon. He had another canteen waiting for me, and I gave him more cigarettes. We kept this up for about ten days until I finally had to call a halt. A liter of wine was a whole bunch for a guy who normally drank one glass a day. I had a continuing buzz on, and my mouth tasted like the inside of an outhouse!

My French, through use, improved markedly. Luigi was an interesting fellow, and I enjoyed the afternoons when I could go up to talk with him. I learned a lot about his life in the army and about his home and family. He was very interested in talking about America, about which he knew nothing. It's hard to describe the magnitude of our country in English, and I'm sure I didn't do it justice in French, but he was impressed. Luigi and I kept up our conversations as often as I was free until I left in June. I used to give him cigarettes every so often, but he seemed uneasy about taking them without giving something in return. Every once in a while, he'd bring in some wine and urge me to take it and I would, to please him.

In March, with the weather so bad, I went to the Exec and asked for a three-day pass to go up to Bari. He OK'd the pass if I'd take some reports up to Fifteenth Air Force Headquarters at Bari. I hitched a ride from Group. Bari was about forty miles northeast of our base. After delivering the papers, I went to the Red Cross, and they fixed me up with a bed for two nights. I didn't know anything about Bari, so I asked the lady what was worth seeing and doing there.

"You should visit the British Officers' Club," she responded. "It's for members only, but they will accept American officers on a short-term basis for $3.00 a day".

She told me how to get there, so I went that evening. It was a very nice place and, compared to our mess hall, a palace. Many of the Brits were there in their bright regimental uniforms--Scots, Welsh Guards, and others I didn't recognize. Talk about peacocks! These guys were wearing long pants with checks so big and patterns so bright I would never dare wear them in public in my home town!

They even had waiters! It was quite a thing to sit in a big chair and have someone bring you a gin and tonic. I stayed around most of the evening. The Brits were not overly friendly to Americans. There were a few of us Yanks there, and we sort of stuck together. I met an Ensign and Commander of a Naval gun crew on a merchant ship anchored in the harbor. We hit it off and, after a few more gin and tonics, he invited me to his mess on the ship for Sunday dinner. He told me how to find the ship, and I promised to be there.

The next morning, I washed, shaved, wiped my shoes, and took off for the ship. I hoped that he would remember me, and he did. I went aboard, and he showed me around the ship. After our tour, he took me down to the wardroom where he and his people ate. I couldn't believe it! White linen tablecloths. Silver service. Fresh roast beef and real potatoes, followed by ice cream for dessert. Compared to his life, we were living like a bunch of poor peasants! He told me that they were resupplied with all the goodies from Navy supply ships that also took care of the regular Navy combat vessels in the area. There was an old saying: "The Navy gets the gravy, and the Army gets the beans". Very true then, and most of us believe it still holds today.

When I got back from Bari, I found that a new regimen had

been put into place the day before. A couple of weeks earlier, a B-24 from another group had exploded and crashed on takeoff just as it broke ground. This was odd because B-24's normally didn't do that. A few nights later, a mechanic working on an airplane noticed a figure moving around a nearby B-24. As the mechanic watched, he saw the figure doing something around one of the main gears. The crew chief started over, and the figure began to run. The chief collared him and marched him into the line shack. It turned out that he was an American airman and he had wired a grenade so that, when the main gear went up, the grenade would explode in the wheel well. He was working for the Germans, and they paid him a large sum for every aircraft he destroyed.

Orders went out to all of the groups to mount guards on all of our airplanes every night. The guard duty fell to all crew members, officers, and EM's alike. It was not pleasant duty. Nights were still cold and there was no comfortable place to sit or lean. Also, there was always a lot going on all night long as ordnance loaded bombs and ammo, gas truck drivers filled tanks, and mechanics arrived in the early hours to "pre-flight" the planes. If you were scheduled for a mission in the morning, you could figure on having to go about twenty-four hours without sleep.

The weather in March was terrible. High winds and driving rain made night guard duty miserable. In fact, the weather caused us to lose our left waist gunner, Carleton Smith. On 16 March 1944, there was a bad storm with very high winds. Fearing for the safety of the airplanes, our operations officer, Rex Thompkins, was down at the parking area firing up the engines and turning the planes into the wind. When he got to the "Chopper", he started the engines and told Smith to remove

111

the ammo box under the tail and then to get out of the way. The B-24' were very delicately balanced, and even the weight of one man back in the tail would frequently cause an airplane to tip down at the back and hit the rudders on the ground. To prevent this, we would stick an ammo box under the tail.

Smith removed the box and started to run to get out of the prop blast. It was pitch black and he thought the airplane was going to turn one way but it turned the other. Running at full tilt, he slammed into one of the large rudders with such force as to break his neck. The medics were called, and they knew that Smith had to be taken to a general hospital immediately for expert medical attention. They rigged a special cot suspended from the walls of the ambulance and immobilized his head the best they could. They then drove him to Bari. Carleton survived, but his flying days were over. I saw him for the first time since then in 1986. He was still feeling the effects of that accident. Over time, his neck size had gone from fifteen to seventeen and a half.

It seemed like March would never end, but it did and with amazing suddenness. One day it was cold and rainy. The next, it turned warm and sunny and the flowers of Italy began to bud and then to bloom. The change took place right with the calendar. April had come.

CHAPTER 15

It's April And We're In The Big Leagues Now

April finally came and with it, much better weather. The group made sixteen missions in April, and our crew got in eight of them. We were now rapidly developing our talents as "professional bombers". The names of our targets were impressive--Steyr, Ploesti, Wiener-Neustadt, Bucharest, Toulon. We ranged all over southern Europe, and our bombing accuracy was some of the best in the Fifteenth Air Force. We began to get replacement airplanes and crews, but we started to lose some of them before we even got to know them well. What really hurt was to see some of our "old hands" shot down. Most of us by the end of April could begin to hope that we might finish our tour--fifty was the magic number. Some were in the thirty's as far as missions were concerned. But, as the targets grew tougher, the odds went down.

April 2, 1944, was Palm Sunday. The raid on Steyr was a rough one although the group lost only three planes. The German fighters were pressing their attacks mostly from the front and sides. They stayed away from the tail quadrant since

Steyr, Austria

"OLD 28"
PALM SUNDAY
1944

"Ye Old Rugged Curse"

115

we were heavily armed there. On the way up to Steyr, a B-24 in front of us was hit and the crew bailed out. Two of the guys came zipping right through our formation, their chutes streaming out behind them. They missed everyone and, I assume, made it OK. It sure was a cold, lonely sight to see them out there over the Alps at twenty-two thousand feet.

At Steyr, we carried "window" for the first time in our theater. The results were spectacular--at least for us. "Window" was what some called "chaff". What it looked like was Christmas tree icicles--strips of lead or aluminum foil in packets which we threw out of the waist windows to confuse the German radar-directed guns. Several groups were in front of us, and their waist gunners were tossing out the "window" as they went down the bomb run and turned off the target. By the time we got to the target, the earlier chaff had drifted off to the side and down. The German gunners were blasting empty air off to the side about a quarter-mile and two or three thousand feet below. We loved it!

Unfortunately, the Germans quickly learned what we were doing. They would start using their radar fire control, but would quickly switch over to optical ranging when they detected us using window. Nonetheless, we still carried big boxes of the stuff every time we could and tossed it out in gay abandon. I rapidly lost faith in its usefulness, however, especially if we were the first over the target and the stuff hadn't had a chance to disperse. I figured it might just attract rather than repel flak in that situation. At Steyr, it worked like a charm, but never again did I personally see it be effective.

On April 4,1944 (the group knows it as "4/4/44"), the 449th went to Bucharest, Romania to bomb the rail yards as a sort of prelude to the attacks on Ploesti, which was thirty miles north. We didn't go, but our tent mates did, and it turned out to be one of the roughest raids our group ever experienced. This was the first raid on Bucharest, and the Germans and Romanians were ready. The flak was bad, but the fighters were the real killers. A hundred or more swarmed all over the twenty-seven B-24's of the 449th, the only group that made it to the target that day because of bad weather. The fighters shot down six B-24's, but our boys were officially credited with shooting down forty German planes and thirteen "probables" that day. They awarded the group one of its two Presidential Unit Citations for that mission.

While the Bucharest mission was on, John got involved in a softball game. As he was trying to field a tough hit, the ball struck his hand right in the pocket between thumb and forefinger and split that skin wide open. John had to get several stitches in his hand, and he was off flying status for several days. Thus, he missed what I believe was the first high-level strike at Ploesti since the low-level attack of August 1943. The rest of us and the "Chopper" went on the mission on 5 April, but the Assistant Operations Officer, Herb Martin, flew as first pilot.

Ploesti is only thirty miles north of Bucharest where the big battle had raged the day before. In fact, our approach to Ploesti on the 5th was to fly almost directly towards Bucharest, turning about ten miles North of the city and heading right up the rail line to Ploesti. This mission was to bust the rail yards at Ploesti, just as we'd done the day before at Bucharest, to prevent shipment of oil to the war fronts. This time, however, there were a number of groups participating and each group was being led by a "pathfinder" (Mickey-radar plane). This

117

was the first time radar was used in the Italian Theater. It wasn't much good, but at least it could "see" major ground features.

We were very, very leery about getting as close to that wasp's nest at Bucharest as we did--the city was clearly visible, and their guns were shooting at us as we approached. However, there were no fighters visible at that point. When we turned, we were right over the rail line and it looked like it would be a clean shot right to Ploesti. Not so at all! We didn't know about the real defenses of Ploesti--those that were more effective than the six-hundred heavy guns and the hundreds of fighters--smoke pots.

As far as I know, Ploesti was the only target in southern Europe that used smoke pots to obscure the target area. They had hundreds of these smoke pots all around the town and the five giant refineries East of town. The Germans had more than two hours warning when we were headed their way. When the pots were lit and smoking, all you could see was a gray pall that obscured everything for miles around. Only if a strong wind were blowing would the pots be ineffective.

We started up the bomb run, and the flak intensified. Fenton was down on his knees, first peering out his observation window and then trying to see something in his bomb sight. I was trying to identify something too, but the closer we got to Ploesti the more obscured things became. We were even losing sight of the rail tracks, which seemed to go into the smoke and disappear. I opened the bomb bay doors when Bob signaled, and we kept on plowing ahead into a torrent of flak bursts. Finally, Fenton looked up.

"I can't see a darned thing through this stuff!" he shouted on the intercom. "I'm going to toggle them. Give me a kick when you see the other planes drop!"

I nodded.

During the bomb run, I used to sit on my navigator's table with my flak vest under my butt and do various things for Fenton such as opening the doors, helping to spot the target, hitting the salvo lever after "bombs away," and closing the doors. He was kneeling just below me, so I kept my foot over his back as I waited for the other planes to drop. Suddenly, one of those flak bursts you always sweat out exploded right outside my window. I could hear the burst and see the flash, and that's close! I jumped, and my foot hit Bob's back. He toggled out ten nicely spaced five-hundred pound bombs. No one else did for what seemed to me the longest minute in my life.

"Why'd you kick me?" Fenton demanded.

"I didn't mean to," I protested. "I jumped at that flak."

We waited and watched, and finally the other planes dropped their bombs, and we rallied off the target.

Fenton was disgusted, but it wasn't all a waste. Our gunners had a fine view to the rear and saw our bombs hit squarely on the tracks and start a pretty good fire--probably a tank car. The raid turned out to be a success, not only in that it destroyed a lot of tank cars and tore up the rail yard at Ploesti, but a number of bombs from the other groups hit in the refinery area to the East and did a lot of damage.

We were in flak for what seemed an eternity. The Ploesti complex was reported to have had over six-hundred heavy guns defending this vital target--one of the three most heavily defended targets of the war, the other two being Berlin and Vienna. Going in the way we did lengthened the time we were under their fire by an extra five minutes to almost twenty minutes--a long time to be a target in that big shooting gallery.

After we got out of the range of the flak batteries, about seventy-five fighters next came charging in--a virtual repeat of the day before. This time the B-24's did it to them with a vengeance! We drove them off and shot down or damaged forty-five of them. The Germans or Romanians who were flying those fighters had taken a terrific beating from the 449th and the rest of the Fifteenth in those two days. The next two times we went to Ploesti there were a lot fewer fighters to contend with.

When we got back, were debriefed, and returned to our squadron area, we thought that we'd had a very lucky mission for such a target as Ploesti. Unfortunately, it was not without a cost. A Co-Pilot named Leonard Resnick had been checked out as a First Pilot. This was his first mission as a First Pilot. When the fighters hit us after the target, a single bullet hit Lennie's plane. It went in through the windshield and struck Lennie in the neck, killing him instantly. He fell forward into the controls, and the plane came out of formation and started down in a turning dive. It dropped for several thousand feet before the Co-Pilot, Bernie Sermersheim, was able to pull Resnick off the controls with one hand while pulling the plane out of its dive--an incredible feat of strength.

Bernie shouted over the intercom for the flight engineer to

120

help him, but the engineer was unable to get Resnick out of the seat. The best he could do was to hold Resnick's body off the controls, which he did for nearly six-hundred miles while they flew home all alone. Bernie brought the plane in and landed it from the right seat. It was an awful experience--with blood all over the controls and blood on everything he had to touch. Bernie got the Silver Star for that feat of airmanship, but the experience just about destroyed him. He kept on flying Co-Pilot until he was finally shot down a month later on another raid on Ploesti. Fortunately, he survived, and he became a POW.

The next day, we took Lennie's body up to the American cemetery at Bari. It was an experience I'll never forget to my dying day. The ambulance, and our truck full of Lennie's friends, pulled up at a building at the cemetery. The head guy rounded up a bunch of his people--Army troops. They took Lennie's body and put it in a pine box and nailed the cover shut. They carried the body to a long trench in which laid out, uncovered, were several other coffins. They put Lennie's box in next to the last one, and there was lots of room for more bodies in the trench.

Up came a firing party and a bugler. Our Chaplain said a few words--a difficult thing for him to do properly since Lennie was Jewish. While that was going on, we friends stood along the trench. I looked over to the next coffin: there was a knothole in the top, and a fly was flying in and out of the hole. There was a faint smell of death in the air. After Father McNamara had finished, the officer called us all to attention, and the firing party fired three volleys. The bugler blew taps, and that was that. It took about fifteen minutes from the time we arrived.

121

Our next mission was into the Vienna area--an aircraft factory complex at Wiener-Neustadt. The Vienna area was always a "hairy" mission, and this one was no exception. Flak was intense and accurate, but we now had P-47's helping on escort, and they kept the fighters off our backs, except for one.

There is courage enough to go around for everyone, friend or foe alike, who flies and fights in the wild blue yonder. One German 109 pilot attacked our twelve-ship formation coming in from the right with his cannon blazing. He shot down the B-24 on the right and kept on going, firing all the time. He passed over us less than fifty feet above us, and everyone who could do so was shooting at him. Harold Nelson, the Bombardier on the new crew in our tent who was flying on our wing, said that we got him, but I'm not so sure. Duck shooters would know how tough it is to hit a bird that flashes over your blind from the side and low. I still remember that black rectangular box, which I believe was an oil cooler, on the belly of the 109 as he screamed by right over my head.

On the 15th, we went back to the marshalling yards at Bucharest. This time it was overcast, and we bombed by "pathfinder" with uncertain results. One thing was different, however. The fighters stayed home and we were not molested.

CHAPTER 16

Twenty-Five Missions--We're Halfway Home

Personally, I did no mission counting in the early days--for two reasons. First, fifty missions seemed so incredibly far to go and, secondly, the chances of making fifty looked really dim. The odds definitely were not in our favor. When I finally toted up my missions after we'd been flying combat three months, I was very surprised to see that the Bucharest raid made eighteen sorties and twenty-five missions. We also added up the group losses in that same time, and they were more than half of the original planes and crews we came over with. Not very comforting statistics! But once you get to twenty-five, you begin to feel a little hope, and you become a mission counter with increasing awareness as you get closer and closer to the magic number, fifty.

April was, in some ways, a watershed month. We began to get replacement planes and crews, and we got the blessed help of the long-range P-51's in keeping the German fighters off our backs.

Spring came early in southern Italy. It turned warm and sunny almost as soon as April began. That's why we were able to fly a lot more missions. It also made living around the squadron a lot more pleasant when we were not flying. Lubin and I undertook a project to enlarge the tent. We got some limestone blocks and laid several courses around the outside edges of the tent. Then, we lifted the canvas sides and stretched them out over the blocks after raising the tent pole in the middle. It gave us quite a bit more room inside, which was good since now we had to put up mosquito netting over each bunk. It was getting to be malaria season, and Doc Conway put us all on Atabrine tablets once a day. His assistant stood beside the chow line and passed out the pills as we passed him.

We were a scruffy lot when not flying, and this was brought home to us vividly early in April. A program had been instituted to swap a few crews between the Eighth and Fifteenth Air Forces--I guess just to let each know how the other half lived. One very warm afternoon, some of us were lounging outside our tents in shorts and skivvies when an Army "6-by" drove up our squadron street kicking up flurries of dust. In the back, dressed to the nines in their Class A uniforms were a Pilot named Rouse and his crew from England. But most amazing of all were the uniforms the officers wore. They were little short jackets that fitted tightly at the waist and had no "blousy" look or patch pockets as the traditional "pinks and greens" had. They looked just great on the guys, and we wondered how come we had never heard of this new uniform.

We learned from them that the jackets were "Eisenhower" or "Ike" jackets, designed personally by Ike and widely copied by all Army troops in England. When you have all of those stars on your shoulders you can design your own uniform with

124

no problem at all. The "Ike" jacket was a fashion revolution!

Rouse reported in, and he and his officers were assigned a vacant tent across the road and up a ways from us. His enlisted men were likewise assigned a tent along enlisted row. At the end of the enlisted row was a shallow pool of water in a small stream--the runoff from the sewer system of the town of Grottaglie, which was about three miles away. This little stream meandered behind our area and then passed under a tiny bridge at the airfield end of our road separating the 718th living area from the airfield itself.

It was hot and humid and, after unloading their baggage and organizing it in their tent, one of the gunners spotted the little pool. He and the others stripped down to their shorts, and, before anyone cold tell them otherwise, they were down cavorting in the pool. The rest of the squadron gunners gaped in amazement. Finally, someone went down and told them that they were bathing in an Italian sewer. They were horrified, but they had to live with it since we had no bathing facilities in our area. They scrubbed themselves down with water from the water supply cart.

Rouse had a way of aggravating all the rest of us by fre- quently assuring us that "that's not the way we did it in the Eighth!" He was particularly critical that we would not fly when the weather was bad at the base or expected to be bad on return. He was used to the beacons and beams that the Eighth had for penetrating clouds. We did not have any of them. He considered our targets to be much inferior to those in the German heartland. I think he regarded his transfer to the Fifteenth as a necessary evil, helped only by the hope that he would by flying easy missions.

Rouse lasted three weeks before he was shot up at Schwecat in the Vienna complex and crash-landed in Yugoslavia on the way home. He and his crew were picked up by the Partisans who got them safely back to Italy in about a month. I suspect that his opinion changed about "milk runs" in the Fifteenth! Vienna was one of the three most heavily defended targets in Europe.

In his short stay with us, Rouse had a couple of other things happen to him that probably confirmed his low opinion of our airmanship. On one mission he flew, he was in the "diamond-down" position in a four-ship element. The tail gunner in the element lead, directly ahead and above Rouse, was charging his guns in preparation for test-firing them-a step done on every mission when we got up at altitude and away from Italy. This time, the tail gunner pulled the charging lever three times instead of twice. This ejected a live fifty-caliber round which dropped out of the tail and struck the Plexiglas nose turret of Rouse's plane. It was cold and the plastic disintegrated in an instant leaving the nose gunner sitting out in the open. Rouse had to abort the mission.

The very next day, Rouse went on another mission flying in the same position. This time, a waist gunner in the back of the element lead plane had the "GI's." Since there was no toilet of any kind in a B-24, the waist gunner emptied a wooden fifty-caliber ammunition box, relieved himself, and then threw the box and its contents out the waist window. The box struck the leading edge of Rouse's left wing and lodged there. Once again, Rouse had to abort. He brought his ship back and landed it with the box still impaled in his wing. Needless to say, there were some very pointed directives from Group about throwing anything out of the airplanes--except bombs.

126

On the 16th of April, we lost the only man on our crew killed in combat. Red Bauers had had a bout with sinusitis and had missed a couple of missions with us. Wanting to catch up, he volunteered to fly a mission to Brasov, Romania, with a replacement crew. Brasov is way out in Romania, about six-hundred miles from our base. There was no escort. They were jumped by German fighters who shot down two B-24's--one of our old crews, Dale Rodgers, and Temchulla's crew with Red aboard as Ball Gunner.

Temchulla's plane was riddled with cannon fire from end to end and was on fire. Most of the crew bailed out immediately, but there was a wounded gunner in the waist. Red somehow got himself out of the ball. He saw the wounded man and, with the plane going down all afire, Red clipped the wounded gunner's chest pack on him, hoisted him to the waist window, and pulled the gunner's rip cord as he pushed him out. The plane blew up, and Red did not get out. How did we know this? The wounded man survived and became a POW. He told the story to the intelligence debriefers when he was repatriated. It's in the Missing Air Crew Reports in the National Archives in Suitland, Maryland. They gave Red the Silver Star--posthumously.

If ever an airplane changed the course of daylight bombardment in Europe, it was the P-51 Mustang escort fighter. We bomber crews before April had to fight our way into and out of every major target in Europe by ourselves. Our losses were enormous from fighter attacks. We tried and tried to destroy German fighter production but to no avail. They outproduced us and were gaining in total sorties against us until mid-April 1944. The P-51's made the difference. They really kept the Germans off our backs and cut our losses tremendously.

It was on a raid on Sofia, Bulgaria, on 17 April 1944 that
we were first escorted by P-51's. The briefing officer told us
about the P-51's and showed us pictures of them. He cautioned us to keep a close eye on them and watch how they did.
Despite all of this, the bomber stream--not our group--shot
down three of them. How could this happen? The P-51, when
you saw it flashing by, looked somewhat like an ME-109. We
had the same problem when they introduced P-47's into our
theater, but they used them differently--as penetration fighters-
-so we usually did not see them close by. They looked like
FW-190's. We had standing instructions to fire at anything that
turned its nose towards us. The P-51 pilots were new and
probably forgot about getting too close to the bombers.

That afternoon, we were called out by the Group Commander to watch a P-51 fly around. A P-51 went to each group
in Italy so that each air crew would get a very good look at our
new "little friends". The pilot who came to our field made
numerous passes over the field, turning in all directions and
coming at us from all points of the compass. His last pass was
supposed to be a low-altitude fly-by right down the runway.
As he came over at full throttle, going probably four-hundred
miles per hour, his canopy blew off. The P-51 veered off its
course and rammed into the skeleton of one of those dirigible
hangars. The plane totally disintegrated. It and the pilot were
scattered all over our field. They picked him up in a burlap
sack.

On the 24th of April, we returned to Ploesti and had another go at the rail yards. What more can one say about
Ploesti? We flew the longest bomb runs used on any target,

128

hoping that the Bombardiers could get a glimpse of the target through the smoke. We were in flak for a good fifteen minutes--almost a lifetime, it seemed, as we just rode along straight and level on a fixed course. As we approached Ploesti, the sky would be darkened with the smoke of flak bursts. You could watch groups literally disappear into this cloud and then come out on the other side. You can't imagine the tension as we approached the cloud knowing what was in it.

When our turn came, the cloud was not as thick as it looked from afar. Now we could watch the individual bursts of flak-- below, to the side, and above. It seemed incredible that we were able to pass through this storm without being destroyed. A lot of guys didn't. Several hundred heavy bombers were shot down over Ploesti during the course of the war. The Romanian prison camps were full of our guys. Our group alone had over ninety men there--the lucky ones who were able to bail out.

This time the fighters didn't get to us. We had both P-38 and P-51 escorts in the area.

I've often been asked, "Weren't you scared on those raids?" The answer, of course, is "Yes!" But, fear affects people in funny ways. When we were being shot at by fighters and flak, all of us were tense and the old adrenalin was pumping. We saw our friends being shot down, but it was like watching a movie. We saw it, but we didn't feel it. We held no post-mortems about their loss--only discussions of how it probably happened. Most of the time, we slept well at night.

I think any guy who flew in bombers hated flak much more than fighters, even though fighters probably did more damage to our formations. I always felt very creepy about seeing flak bursts right above us. How did they get up there? Even more worrisome, sometimes we could pick out flak batteries on the ground firing at us. It would take nearly twenty seconds for those shells to reach our altitude of twenty-five thousand feet. I'd wonder if I were looking at the shell being fired that was going to get us.

My worst time in all my flying came on a raid on the submarine pens at Toulon, France. This was a long seven-hour mission, but not much to worry about until we got to the target itself. We were out over the water most of the time. When we got to Toulon, the flak was very heavy. And we were facing a different kind of flak--very large bursts of grayish brown color instead of the smaller, black flak bursts from 88's, the German's favorite weapon. This big stuff turned out to be shells from French Naval anti-aircraft guns captured by the Germans. Those great big bursts were exploding one-thousand to two-thousand feet directly above us. How those shells missed us on the way up I'll never know. A hit would blow a B-24 to pieces. It seemed that we were in their range forever.

I sweated and shook most of the way home, calming down only after we had landed. I felt awful in my stomach. Later that evening, shortly after supper, I began to shake again. I couldn't control it, and John and Fenton half carried me over to Doc Conway's medical tent. Doc covered me up in blankets and gave me some sort of a pill and a drink. I stayed there until about eleven PM trying to calm down and get the memory of those flak bursts out of my mind. I told him that I didn't think I could face that again. Doc told me, "OK, if you feel that way in the morning, I'll ground you for a few days."

When morning came and John and the rest got ready to go, I had to go with them, and I did. Happily, this was a "milk run" to a town called Allesandra. We missed the target almost completely, and the Germans only fired a few very inaccurate rounds at us. Believe me, I needed that.

One other thing happened in April that is so bizarre that only pictorial evidence will confirm what I'm about to relate. The picture of the whole crew standing beside the Chopper taken at Topeka just before we left for overseas shows the nose art that we had painted on at Bruning. We were very proud of our design. It was unique and went with the name "Wood's Chopper". Now, near the end of April, there was a 47th Wing inspection team that visited our base. The wing inspectors were looking over all of the airplanes. When they saw the "Chopper", they ordered Muller, our crew chief, to paint out the two heads and the block, leaving only the upraised arm with its ax and the name. The reason?

"So as not to offend the enemy," they said.

We were flabbergasted. If the Germans were not already offended by our bombing them twenty-five times and shooting down their fighters, surely a little nose art wouldn't disturb them! Never-the-less, we flew the rest of our missions in the "Chopper" with a white patch on our nose, as the picture of her assembling for a raid in May, 1944 will attest.

"Wood's Chopper" - May 1944

CHAPTER 17

My Faith Looks Up To Thee

May began and nearly ended for the "Chopper" and her crew on the 5th. It was Ploesti again, and this time it was a "maximum effort" on the part of the Fifteenth to finally knock out the oil facilities and the marshalling yards at one time. It didn't happen, but we gave it a heck of a shot. There were sixteen groups on that raid in two bomber streams. This would be about five-hundred planes--the biggest raid we'd ever mounted to date. The 449th was chosen to lead this massive armada, and the 718th Squadron was the lead squadron. Bob Fenton, our own Bombardier, was the lead bombardier. The squadron navigator was leading, and why the squadron bombardier wasn't on the bombsight I don't know, but Fenton was chosen and rightly so. He was good.

John and the rest of us in the "Chopper" were flying deputy lead--a nice place to be in some respects because it made flying formation much easier. A Bombardier named Van Sickle took Fenton's place; otherwise, the crew was intact.

Smoke Pots, Ploesti

(449BG:4M54:3VI)(5·05·1359)(24:21200)(20°T)PLOESTI M.Y. Ship #34

Ploesti, Romania

We took the usual long flight across Yugoslavia and into Romania. We approached Ploesti from the West and reached our IP just about on schedule--at noon. It was a fine, clear day at our altitude--twenty-three thousand feet. It was an amazing sight to look back and see hundreds of contrails streaking the skies for as far as you could see. If I were a Romanian, I would be heading for the shelters. Someone was due for a real pasting.

We were on an unusually long bomb run, even for Ploesti-- about twenty-five miles. Our group was visually bombing since we had no "pathfinder" equipment. As usual, the smoke pots were obscuring the whole area except near the town. Fenton found a clear spot, however, and used it as an aiming point. When he dropped, we dropped, and so did the rest of our group.

Before that raid was over, more than twelve-hundred tons of five-hundred pound bombs--five-thousand of them--fell on the yards and on the refinery area. With that kind of tonnage, there had to be some serious damage, and there was. Fires raged, and black smoke rose quickly hundreds of feet into the air. At last! We could report some damage! As it turned out, we did much better than we thought. Intelligence reported from reconnaissance flights the next day that seventy-five percent of the refinery facilities were damaged or destroyed and the rail yards were a mess--not all due to this raid but to the accumulated result.

The Germans fought back ferociously. This time, because we were up front, there was no question about who the Germans were aiming at. It was at us. They combined two tactics at Ploesti, barrage firing and aimed shooting. Some of their gunners would simply blast away into an area or "box" of air, hoping we would run into it. The other gunners, using radar-controlled guns, would zero in on individual planes or tightly grouped elements. We were on this bomb run for nearly ten minutes, straight and level, and all I had to do was watch and sweat. After we rallied off the target, we continued in the flak for another five to seven minutes. As soon as we cleared that, the fighters jumped us. It was important for them to get the lead ships, if possible.

We had quite a fire fight, although it seemed to me that there were a lot fewer fighters than previously. Up front where we were, we never did see any of our fighter escort that was supposed to be there. I guess with five-hundred planes to watch over they couldn't be everywhere. There just weren't that many P-51's in the whole theater. Our attackers finally left us to go after the cripples. Unfortunately, there were some. The 449th lost four B-24's in the target area that day.

We began a slow descent, crossing the Danube at the "Iron Gate" at about twelve-thousand feet. I never saw any "gate" and still don't know what the "Iron Gate" was or is. There is a big bend in the Danube near that point. Also, the Danube is NOT blue, or at least it wasn't on the several times I saw it. It was dirty brown like most rivers in the spring.

At this point, things began to go dreadfully wrong. We had been briefed on en-route flak batteries and told to be sure to take a course ten miles north of the Bor chrome mines because there were an estimated four guns there. Our lead navigator apparently was lost, although how that could happen was and is impossible for me to understand. The bend in the Danube was as clear as a bell, and Bor was only about thirty-five miles beyond in the mountains. The hills were probably six-thousand feet high, and we were at twelve-thousand feet--a range of six -thousand feet for the German gunners.

I called John on the interphone. "John, we're headed right for those mines they briefed us on!" I said. "If that idiot doesn't start turning soon, we'll be right over them!"

John would not break radio silence to call the lead plane. Instead, he got on the interphone. "Pilot to crew," he said. "Listen up, now. We're headed for some mines that are supposed to have some flak guns down there. Everyone put on your flak vests and helmets and look alive. Keep your chutes handy!" We did.

I couldn't believe we were doing this to ourselves. We kept right on the same course, same altitude, same speed. It seemed like we waited forever, and I was just beginning to hope that I was wrong when it happened.

Four bursts of flak hit right in the midst of our lead element of four planes. I was looking out my side window when they hit. Paul Harper, in the "diamond-down" position, suddenly swing up wildly on a wing and disappeared behind us. Just a few seconds later, his plane came back into view and slammed into a mountain. A great big hole appeared in the trailing edge and aileron of the lead plane, and one of his gear dropped down. The left wing man swung out of formation and then slowly closed again. It was obvious that something was badly wrong with him. And the "Chopper"--the flak rattled through her like hail.

It was all over after that one salvo. We were so close to the

138

guns that we were beyond their tracking in just a few seconds. We took off our chutes and helmets, and John asked, "You all OK?"

We all reported OK, but Ayers. He was down in the bomb bay trying desperately to staunch a spray of gasoline that was spurting out of one of the cross-feed lines. It had been cut by flak. Finally, he got one of the waist gunners to help, and they broke the line and stuffed chewing gun in both ends. He went up on the flight deck and told John not to use any radio equipment to avoid sparks. Everything, including Ayers, reeked of gasoline. We couldn't even use the "put-put" on landing, for fear of explosion.

I went up on the flight deck since we were below oxygen level. Van Sickle pointed to Lubin's windshield. A piece of flak had come through the window, passed right between Lubin's body and his arm, hit the arm rest, missed Van Sickle's leg by a hair, hit the armor plate behind John, and then lodged itself in John's seat cushion. John still had that piece of flak after forty-one years. When we got back to base, we discovered that flak had hit the oil coolers on three of our engines. They had to change them.

The lead plane in which Fenton was riding crash-landed on our field and was scrapped. Our wing man, Dave Rasbach, had one man killed and two others wounded. And that lead navigator called the rest of us navigators together and tried to get us to say he was on course and that we didn't go over Bor. We walked out on him, and he never flew lead again.

I thought that Paul Harper and his crew were all killed when their plane went into the mountain. In early October of

1944, I was an instructor navigator at Charleston Army Air
Base. We did a lot of night instruction, and I would eat at the
mess hall when we got back--about 5AM. I had finished
eating one morning and was coming out of the mess hall, just
at dawning, when who should be coming up the steps, but Paul
Harper. It was like seeing a ghost.

Paul and his entire crew had bailed out in those few seconds
when I couldn't see their plane. They were very low and hit
the ground right away. Nine of them landed on one side of a
river. They were picked up by a Chetnik group who treated
them kindly and, after about ninety days, got them back to
Italy. The tenth man, Bernie Sermersheim, the Co-Pilot who
was with Len Resnick when he was killed, landed on the other
side of the river, broke his ankle, and was captured by the
Germans.

Dave Rasbach and what was left of his original crew were
taken off flying status after that mission and sent home. He
had been shot up badly so many times that everyone agreed
that forty-three missions were enough for them. It really began
to hurt us original crews to see our old friends with mission
numbers in their forty's getting shot down. Harper's crew
were also over forty when they went down.

That night, as I lay in my bunk unable to sleep, I did
something I had never done before. I prayed to God. My
prayer was very simple because I was not a religious person
then. I said, "God, give me my life, and I will never ask for
anything else again." He did, and I have never asked for
anything--not material goods, not wealth, not position, not
power--only to look out for my wife and family and to help me
to understand what He would want of me. After I had prayed,

140

I somehow knew that I was going to be OK. Though I flew a number of other missions--and some of them were rough--I never again felt the fear that I had experienced before that night. Further, my life since then has been sometimes hectic, but never fearful. I have had everything I ever wanted, and I know for sure that God loves me.

CHAPTER 18

We Entertain Some Visitors

May continued and we slowly moved up in mission numbers. And our losses continued, although not at the earlier rate. We lost Hank Silvers on his forty-fifth mission at a place called Orbetello on the west coast of Italy. The Germans were getting desperate to move supplies because the Italian rail net was mostly destroyed. There was an island close in to the coast, and a causeway connected it to the mainland at Orbetello. The Germans would bring in supplies at night by sea and then haul them over the causeway to the mainland and then move them by truck. We went up and bombed the causeway and its choke point --a really great example of pinpoint bombing.

It should have been a "milk run," but Orbetello was a German anti-aircraft gunners school and the instructors were outstanding shootists. The flak was deadly--intense and accurate. Hank was hit in one wing, and it folded over the top all afire. Five guys got out including their replacement Navigator and Charlie Foskett, the Bombardier. When they got to the ground, two of the gunners and the Navigator tried to escape.

Piacenza, Italy

Orbatello, Italy

The Germans cut them down with machine-gun fire. They made Charlie and the other gunner carry in the bodies to the German headquarters. Eventually, Charlie wound up in the same prison camp as Colonel Alkire. Charlie said he hadn't changed a bit. When he reported to him, Charlie started to tell him about how he had gotten shot down. Alkire waved it aside.

"Never mind that," he growled, "What's happening to the group?" he demanded.

As May progressed, it got hot. No more afternoon naps in the tent, and the heat held on--even at night. We were able, however, to roll up the tent sides to get more air, but that resulted in a two-week visit from one of the most obnoxious little villains we had ever met--all two pounds of him.

Some of the guys on the way over bought monkeys from kids selling them in Brazil. Several of them died en route, but one belonging to a pilot named Stewart survived. Stewart rapidly tired of him and tossed him out to fend for himself. He did, by wandering all over the squadron area, visiting different tents, and scrounging anything he could find. He ate mostly at the rear of the mess hall where the cooks gave him scraps. The things he really loved, however, were candy and gum, and those he could only get from the tents.

At first we thought he was cute and he was. We got a real kick out of handing him a bar of candy or a stick of gum in the wrapper and watching his little hands unwrap it and stuff it in his mouth. Later, when we would be out of the tent, the little bugger would open our footlockers and get the candy and gum for himself. If we tried to hide it under our clothes in the footlocker, he'd pull everything out to get at the goodies. The only way to keep him out was to lock them--an inconvenience for us.

His unpopularity grew with every day's performance. Sometimes, he would go on a tear as though he were demented. He would leap up on the top bunks and then jump into the mosquito netting, making a tangled mess of it. We'd chase him around the tent, but he'd mostly outrun us or he'd simply jump out onto the outside walls of the tent and sit there jabbering at us. If anyone ever caught him, as we occasionally did, he'd pee on his captor or on his bunk--which was worse. It was very clear why Stewart had banished that hyper little terror.

We despaired of getting free of him because we had no way of keeping him out. Finally, Harold Nelson found the magic cure. Tents like the ones we lived in had an air flap at the top-- a piece of canvas with a rope attached to it and secured to the tent pole. The purpose of the rope was simply to close the flap if it were raining. One night, that miserable little creature had done his usual act of violence on the mosquito-netted bunks. Then, he jumped up on our table and ran up the tent pole and sat on the rope which formed a sort of loop near the top of the tent. This was a strategic mistake on his part.

"Aha, you little bastard, I've got you now!" Nelson shouted as he pulled out his Zippo and set the bottom of the rope on fire.

As the fire crept slowly up the rope like a fuze, the monkey got more and more agitated. He was jabbering and showing his teeth and shifting his footing on the rope loop. When the

Marseilles, France

Wollersdorf Airdrome, Vienna, Austria

fire finally reached the bottom of the loop where it was attached to the tent pole, our little tormentor had had enough. He sprung out of the hole in the roof and disappeared and we never saw him again. What a relief!

We were bombing now with a level of expertise that made us know we were winning this war, hands down. The prettiest raid we flew in May was on the 27th when we bombed the St. Charles railway station right in the heart of Marseilles, France. This was a long range flight from Grottaglie--over twelve hundred miles round-trip. But, it was a fine clear day and mostly over water. When we got to the target, the whole situation was perfect for bombing. The station was easily recognizable, and the flak was not particularly intense, nor accurate. The 449th was first over the target so Fenton had a nice aiming point--the train station itself. The bombing was so precise that the station and yards were totally destroyed and only a few bombs fell outside the target area. Best of all, we didn't lose a plane.

The military powers that be, in their infinite wisdom, thought it would be a morale booster for the infantry to send some of their guys on an Air Corps mission, just to observe what we were doing for the war effort. In earlier days during the terrible winter of '43-'44, they used to route us bombers across Italy--just inside the Allied lines and at about six-thousand feet--so that the troops could see that they were not alone, I guess. Now, they wanted an infantry guy to experience a real mission, and an Army Major flew with us on the 29th of May on a mission to Wiener-Neustadt.

Things were a lot easier up around Vienna than in the earlier days. We had lots of fighter escort--P38's, P-51's, and

150

for good measure P-47's. These latter fighters went in ahead of us and shot up the flak batteries. They didn't get them all, by a long shot, because the flak was at least as bad around those aircraft plants, if not worse. The Fifteenth Air Force was purely professional now, and we did a number on an aircraft plant and its adjacent airdrome. We were not first over the target, and when we got there it was partially obscured by the bomb hits of the front groups. We put our bombs right into the midst of the previous hits, and that target was kaput!

The flak had been intense and accurate. The group lost two B-24's to flak, I think. Our own fighters were all over the place, and the forty or so German fighters that rose to meet them were heavily engaged and didn't have much chance at the B-24's.

After we got down below oxygen altitude, I crawled out of the nose and went up on the flight deck as I usually did. The Army Major sat there on the deck. He still had on his flak vest, helmet, and parachute. I sat down beside him.

"You can take that stuff off now, Major," I said. "We're OK." He did. "Well, what did you think of the mission?" I asked.

The Major shook his head.

"You guys must be crazy to do this! I felt like a sitting duck--no, a moving duck in a shooting gallery! I've never seen so many rounds aimed right at us. Don't you realize those are '88 shells? Do you know what one of those things would do to this airplane if it hit it?"

151

"Yeah, we know," I answered. "But remember two things, We're only in this stuff for ten or fifteen minutes and secondly, if we are hit, we have these." I pointed to his chute.

"Personally, I don't know how you guys on the ground can stand being under fire for days with all sorts of guns shooting at you. You live in holes like animals, cold, wet, and probably hungry. I can't imagine hearing shells come screaming in and exploding all around me. We usually don't hear anything."

"I still have a hole to duck into," he responded with finality.

"Chacun a son gout!" as the French say--to each his own!.

CHAPTER 19

It's June And It's Over

I started June with forty-two missions done and eight to go, but it took almost the whole month to get those eight. The forty-third mission was to a marshalling yard at Simeria, Romania, on 2 June. It was a lousy mission from the standpoint of bombing, but it was a good one for a guy who was getting increasingly "flak happy." There was only light, inaccurate flak and no fighters. On the 5th, we went to Bologna, Italy, and made "bologna" out of their marshalling yard. The 5th was also the day we took Rome. On that day, there was a maximum effort on all of the rail yards in Italy to interrupt the flow of men and supplies to the Germans, who were in full retreat. It only took one group to wipe out a railroad marshalling yard, so the Fifteenth spread out over all of northern Italy and we hit lots of targets that day.

On the 11th, two things happened - we made our longest raid and we all got promoted.

The target on the 11th was Constanta, Romania--a massive

Constanta, Romania

oil tank farm way out on the Black Sea about seven-hundred and fifty miles from our base. We carried two-hundred and fifty pound bombs, which proved to be a big mistake. When we got to Constanta, the target was clear and it looked like a zillion nice, fat oil tanks. The flak was moderate and we saw no fighters. Still, we lost one plane from the group. The bombing was good but the results weren't. The tanks were each surrounded by revetments, and the two-hundred and fifties were just not powerful enough to breach them. Many tanks were hit, but it didn't wipe out the farm as we had hoped after flying all that distance. This was Ayer's final mission. We had a new Flight Engineer after that.

Orders were waiting for us when we got back promoting John to Captain and Fenton, Lubin, and me to First Lieutenants. I think the total pay raise was $50.00 per month including flight pay. This brought us up to $275.00 per month-- certainly more money than we could begin to spend over in Italy.

The big problem for us new First Lieutenants was to find silver bars. There had been a lot of promotions lately as guys finished up their missions, and silver bars were in short supply. John gave Fenton and me each, one of his two sets which he no longer needed. The rest had to take blitz cloths to their gold bars and rub like hell to get the brass off to expose the silver underneath.

I dreaded the look of the briefing map on the 13th. It ran way, way up into Germany to Munich, a target we knew was a toughie, even though our group had never been there. Munich was usually an Eighth Air Force target, but this time the Fifteenth got the honors. We carried the new thermite fire bombs-

-the little hexagonal sticks bundled together in bunches that ignited fires almost impossible to put out. Obviously, some one else was going before us to make the kindling.

The raid turned out better than I expected. We had good fighter protection. A number of groups had preceded us, and the target had been pounded. The flak was really bad. Munich was one of the more heavily protected cities in Germany, and the Germans did their best to defend it. In spite of the tremendous flak barrages, we didn't lose a single plane over Munich. We also had a nice view of Salzburg and of Berchtesgaden, Hitler's retreat, on the way home.

On the 14th, we hit another oil storage target, at Osijek, Yugoslavia. This was just what the doctor ordered--a "milk run" with no flak, no fighters, and a lovely fire started by our bombs that insured Hitler wouldn't get any of that oil.

Now, at this point, I had forty-eight missions, and I was holding my breath. Just two more. I decided that I wouldn't write any more letters home until I could tell my folks and my girl that I was coming home.

Well, a funny thing happened on the way to fifty--the weather turned rotten. We were briefed for several missions and got all ready to go, only to have them canceled. Now, this really grates on one's nerves. It was eight days before we finally got off a mission--a railroad bridge at Latisana. The weather over the target was totally undercast and we didn't drop, but the mission counted since we went over the target. That was number forty-nine. I counted it with pleasure.

The weather continued bad--almost as bad as it had been in

March. Nothing on the 23rd, nor the 24th. And then the 25th came, and the target, of all things, was the sub pens at Toulon-- the one place I dreaded more than all others. We had a round trip of twelve-hundred miles, and the enroute weather was marginal. I'm surprised that they didn't call it off, but we went all the way. The target was totally obscured. The only way we could even tell we were there was by the few big flak bursts of those big shells from the naval guns. We dropped on the lead ship, but heaven knows what we hit. Later, we learned that most of the bombs had fallen in the city.

Well, that was number fifty. Now to get home. The weather got worse and worse as we tried to let down. Soon, the group broke up into its individual flights and, in some cases, into elements and individual planes. It is no fun flying in dense clouds with a lot of other airplanes in there with you.

Our flight got down to seven planes with us leading. We stuck together loosely and, when we got down to about eight-thousand feet, we found a few breaks in the clouds. I saw the coast of Italy momentarily and, by great good fortune, saw a place that matched one on my map. I'd been dead reckoning from Toulon, and I badly needed a visible checkpoint to set the course for home. I laid out the line and gave John a course and an ETA. As we neared the ETA, John began to let down gradually, and the rest followed. Suddenly, at about four-thousand feet, we broke out--right over the Bay of Taranto.

I crawled out of the nose and went up on the flight deck. I stood behind John and Lubin and watched as John made his turn for the field. Finally, after the rest had landed, our turn came.

"John," I said, "do it nice for me, please."

"Eephus," he grinned, "you won't even feel it!"

He was right. He made a "kiss" landing--just a little squeak as the wheels touched. He taxied over to our stand and shut off the engines. Finally, everything was quiet. They let me get out first. Never did I feel so much alive. Never did the earth and all of the surroundings look so bright and sharp. I had my life, for whatever purpose it was meant to be. I thanked God.

John needed one more mission for his fiftieth. Instead, he drew a double-credit mission, to Swechat in the Vienna complex. Nosker offered to pass him by on that one, but John said no, he'd go. I sweated him out all day on the ground, but the "Chopper" came home, and John was all done, with fifty-one missions.

We just hung around the area for a few days while they got the paper work together. We were all done except Lubin, who had been checked out as a First Pilot after his forty-fifth mission and was flying his own crew in another plane. Finally, he finished, and that was all of us. On the 30th, I was designated as the courier to take a bunch of orders of guys who had finished their missions, along with ours, up to Fifteenth Air Force Headquarters at Bari.

I was up there three days getting the orders for home cut. On July 3rd, I arrived back at the base. As I came into our area, I saw an odd sight. Over our tent on a long tether was a balloon. When I got to the tent and greeted the guys, I found out why. The "Chopper" had crashed the day before, trying to

158

land with a replacement crew after being hit at Budapest. The balloon was from the emergency radio set which we carried in case we went down over water. The balloon was filled with hydrogen to hoist an antenna. It was the last and only memorial to the "Chopper", serial number 42-7750. It had happened one week after we had finished with her.

CHAPTER 20

We Journey Back To Reality

John, Lubin, and I--and several other guys from other crews--left Grottaglie on 5 July in a B-24 bound for Naples. It was a relaxed festive flight because we were only passengers on the first leg of our trip home. We all were sitting on the flight deck and we kept getting up to see if we could spot Vesuvius, which was one of our favorite landmarks. Finally, there she was, still spouting smoke. The pilot began to let down, and we all cautioned him to do it right--"grease" her in. He did, and we cheered. Now, we would be changing our mode of transportation--a pleasant ocean voyage, we hoped.

A "Six-by" hauled us and our baggage about five miles out of Naples to what was known as "the race track"--built in Mussolini's hey-day, but now a famous replacement depot, or "repo-depo," as we called it. The race track area was a sea of tents. Soldiers of many divisions were there, some going home, some coming into Italy as replacements and scheduled for the front, and some on a short break from combat. There were also, like us, many fliers of bombers and fighters waiting to depart for home. We were processed in and assigned to tents without regard as to who or what we were, so John, Lubin, and I were split up and assigned different tents. It took several hours to find each other after we had gotten settled.

One of my tent mates turned out to be a Lieutenant from the Thirty-Sixth Division who had been with that outfit from North Africa on: Sicily, Salerno, and Anzio--some of the bitterest fighting of the war. Another was a P-47 Pilot. Neither of these guys was very enthusiastic about B-24 people. The infantry guy had been bombed by us when some of our bombs dropped short at Anzio. He later admitted that the "heavies," as we were called, may just have saved the beachhead on the 20th of February when we virtually wiped out a whole Panzer division located in a woods and getting ready for a massive attack.

Like all fighter pilots, the P-47 jockey was highly incensed that the bombers which he was supposed to be protecting would shoot at him if he strayed too close to them. I told him the rules we followed, and he somewhat grudgingly admitted that he knew those rules too, but sometimes got a little careless. We made up our differences and became good friends for the time we were together. I was very much in awe as I listened to the Infantry officer tell about ground combat. I couldn't believe men could stand that sustained fighting and shelling for days on end. At least our fighting was for a few hours at a time, and then back to our safe base and warm bed. He had been at it off and on for nearly two years.

We had no idea when we would get a ship to take us home. No one told us anything. We only had to sign out at the depot orderly room to go into Naples, and we did, frequently. Naples

162

was a big, dirty city. The dock area had been badly bombed and some bombs had fallen in the city to complicate the mess.

We found out very quickly that the permanent party, rear-echelon people "ran" Naples. They had grabbed all of the decent living accommodations, and many of them were set up in "housekeeping" arrangements with local girls. Their Officers' Clubs were restricted to members only and we couldn't even get in to have a drink. They had MP's out on the prowl to grab any enlisted man who dared to come into Naples without a tie. They warned us officers but, unless things got nasty, they let us go. We despised the whole lot of them. They were called the Peninsular Base Section (PBS), and we thought they were a disgrace to the American Army--not only in the way they lived, but in the way they treated the combat troops--ground and air.

One place we could get into was the Orange Club, an all-services club up on a high hill overlooking Naples and the bay. It was a beautiful place reached by a funicular or cog railway--a very steep ascent. The Orange Club had been a German Officers' Club, and the same band that had played for the Germans played for us. The favorite song was Lili Marlene--the old German drinking song that became the marching song for the Afrika Corps. We got those Italians to play it over and over again. I'll bet by the end of the war they hated it!

It was thirteen days before they called our names to be briefed for the trip home on the boat. Before we were loaded, they told us that we were to turn in everything we'd been issued or had acquired that was Army property. They told us that there would be a "showdown" inspection before we could disembark in the States and, if they found any GI material which was not our authorized property, we'd be sent directly back to Italy. It was amazing how many weapons, knives, binoculars, and watches were turned in! Of course, there was no such "showdown" when we reached the States, but no one was going to take a chance on that.

The boat was a Victory ship--one of those cargo or troop ships that were turned out in the shipyards every two weeks. Our accommodations were minimal--rubber bunks stacked five deep--no sheets, but a simple pillow. There were several latrines, but not as many as there should have been for the number of people using them. Showers were cold saltwater. We did have fresh, hot water to wash and shave in. Feeding was "by the numbers", each meal having three or four seatings. The food was of marginal quality.

The hold was hot and stuffy in the July heat in Naples Bay. It didn't get much better when we finally put out to sea the next day. I did most of my sleeping at night, up on the rear cargo hatch where I could get a little breeze. It was noisy, but a lot better than down in the hold.

It took us eighteen days from the time we boarded in Naples to reach port at Newport News, Virginia. The last two days were a nightmare for us passengers and not much better for the crew, I guess. A hurricane had passed up the East Coast of the United States as we were approaching. The ocean swells were enormous. The damned boat rolled and pitched all over the place, and you never saw so many deathly sick people in your life.

The last night out, they tried to draft a party to clean up the forward latrine. I was one of those chosen. We were given

164

mops, brooms, and buckets, and we went in. The scene was like something from Hell. Someone had his head down each toilet, retching horribly. The floor was a stinking mess. I took one look and that was enough. I just managed to get on deck and reach the rail and everything went. I figured they'd never find me among all that chaos and I was right. I don't know who cleaned up that latrine, but it wasn't me.

We pulled up to the dock at Newport News, Virginia in the late afternoon of the 2nd of August. Everyone was feeling much better, and we greeted enthusiastically the few hospitality girls who were there to welcome us. Some of the more raucous troops were waving chocolate bars and shouting "Chocolate!" "Chocolate!" It had worked magic in Italy, but not now in the U.S.

They took us by train to Camp Patrick Henry for the night. They sorted us out as to destination, and the next day a goodly bunch of us boarded a train for Fort Devens, Massachusetts. We arrived in the afternoon of the 3rd of August. They told us to get a good night's sleep because they were going to get us up early in the morning and process us out so we could go home on leave. They said that if everyone did exactly as he was told, we'd be out of there by 10:30 in the morning. And we were. At about 10:15 A.M., I found myself standing outside the processing building with orders in my hand giving me twenty-one days leave and one day travel time. The problem was that this was Ayer, Massachusetts, in the center of the state, and I needed to get to Brockton, Massachusetts, down near the South Shore.

I was not alone. Several other guys gathered around, and we found that the next bus for Boston wouldn't leave until

2 P.M. We couldn't wait, so four of us hired a cab for the hour-long trip to Boston. We had the money, and it was the first money we'd spent since we got home. We all agreed that the driver should take us to the Copley Plaza--a hotel in the center of Boston and close to all other transportation. We got there about 11:45 A.M. and went in to the famous "Merry-Go-Round-Bar"--a bar that slowly rotated as you sat there and the first rotating bar most of us had ever seen. We each had one drink. We were all hyper about finally going home, and one drink was plenty. We broke up the party, bidding each other goodby and heading off in our separate ways.

CHAPTER 21

The Soldier Home From The Wars

It was noon on the 4th of August, 1944. I was still twenty miles from home so I decided to call my Dad and tell him where I was and ask him to come pick me up. I hadn't written home for over a month so no one knew I was anywhere about. I went to a pay phone in the lobby and called my home. No answer. They were out somewhere.

"Well," I decided, "I'll take the subway to Ashmont and call again."

Shouldering my musette bag and picking up my B-4, I got the subway and rode it to the end of the line at Ashmont. When I came up to the surface, there, just about to depart, was the bus to Brockton. I jumped aboard. A half-hour later I was in downtown Brockton. There was a bus every ten minutes that stopped at the foot of my street. No sense in calling now. I waited for it to come, and boarded the bus marked "Montello." Fifteen minutes later, there I was in front of the Waldo Market, where my parents bought their groceries, at the foot of Hillcrest Avenue.

I got off and went into the market. The owner was amazed to see me because, just an hour before, my Father had been in there and had said that he hadn't heard a word from me for several weeks and had no idea when I'd be coming home. I talked with the guys for a few minutes and then called home. My Dad answered. He was very surprised, but he said he'd be right there.

I was standing outside the market when he drove up. He grabbed me and hugged me, and he was crying. I was embarrassed because I'd never seen my Father cry before. I said, "Let's go home, Dad," and I threw my bags in the back seat. We were home in less than five minutes and my Mother was at the door. Ma didn't cry, but I knew she wouldn't. She was old New England stock and they don't cry much.

We all went in and sat down in the living room. They were both trying to tell me everything about all of my friends and the neighbors--things that were important to them and which they thought were important to me. I more or less just listened and thought how good it was to be home. I wanted to talk about the last year--the most important year in my life. But, it came to me in a flash of comprehension: there was no way they would understand. They had never even ridden in an airplane and probably didn't even know what a B-24 looked like. How could I ever explain to them about flak and fighters and fear and death at twenty-five thousand feet? So, we talked about things we could all relate to for almost two hours. Finally, I arose.

"Ma," I said, "I've got to take a bath and get cleaned up.

I'm as filthy as a pig."

I took my bags up to my room--it was just the way I had remembered it. Not a thing had changed. I unzipped my B-4 bag and took out my Class A uniform and hung it in the closet. I hung my hat on the chair post. I got out the one set of "suntans" that were still reasonably clean and laid them on the bed. I got out the dirty uniforms and the used underwear, socks, and handkerchiefs and put them all in the big old chair by the bed. Ma would find them and wash them for me.

I took a long warm bath and then I shaved. I put on the clean clothes and stood in front of the mirror tying my tie. Now that I was back in the States, that was required. When I was dressed, I reached over for my "fifty-mission" hat and put it on. I looked at myself in the mirror. There I was, twenty-two years old--a "lean, mean fighting machine!" I gave my old hat just a little more tilt.

Then, I borrowed my Dad's car and went to see my girl.

POSTSCRIPT

In the first six months of operations in Italy, the 449th Bomb Group lost sixty-three B-24's in combat.

Of the seventeen crews of the 718th Squadron who trained together at Bruning, Nebraska, from September to November 1943, ten were shot down in the first six months of operations.

INDEX

Air Transport Command (ATC) 18

Alkire, Col Darr H. 4, 7, 64, 69, 71, 76, 146

Allesandra, Italy 131

Atkinson Field, British Guiana 21

Atlas Mountains, Morocco 37

Aviano, Italy 72, 76

Axis Sally 94, 95, 106

Ayers,Sgt Wilfred xiv, 5, 139

Bari, Italy 53, 90, 109, 121

Bauers, Sgt Dennin "Red" 44, 72, 127

Belem, Brazil 21

Bologna, Italy 153

Borinquin Field, Puerto Rico 19

Bor Chrome Mines, Yugoslavia 137

Bradley, 2nd Lt. Gilbert 101

Brasov, Romania 127

Brockton, Mass. 3, 100, 167

Bruning Army Air Base, Nebraska 3, 8

Bucharest, Romania 116, 122

Camp Patrick Henry, Virginia 165

Chandler, 2nd Lt. Thomas 49, 53, 75

Clovis, New Mexico 3

Constanta, Romania 153

Conway, Dr. William (Flt. Surgeon) 81, 124, 130
Councill, Capt. David 38
Dakar, West Africa 27, 35
Drinan, 2nd Lt. Edward 101
Fortalaza, Brazil 23, 25, 26
Fort Devens, Mass. 165
Downey, Lt. Col. Richard xiii
Fenton, 2nd Lt. Robert xiv, 5, 59, 118, 133
Foskett, 2nd Lt. Charles 143
Grankowski, Sgt. William xiv
Graz, Austria 101
Green, Col. Hershell 100
Grottaglie, Italy 45, 82
Harper, 2nd Lt. Paul 138, 139
Haizlip, Lt. Col. William 8
Hansen, Sgt. Robert 70
Ihrie, 1st Lt. Peter 53
Isgrigg, 2nd Lt. Vincent 70
Kendall, 2nd Lt. Ben 75
Kneis, Sgt. Norbert xiv
Latizana, Italy 156
Livingston, 2nd Lt. David 53, 74
Lubin, 2nd Lt. Sylvan xiv, 5, 19, 26, 32, 44, 47, 48, 85, 139
Maison Blanche Airport, Algeria 40
Manduria, Italy 94
Marrakech, Morocco 36, 39
Marseilles, France 150
Martin, 2nd Lt. Herbert 117
McNamara, Father Thomas 63, 121
Morrison Field, West Palm Beach, Fla 15
Mostar, Yugoslavia 5, 67
Muller, Sgt Robert xiv, 11, 35, 63

Munich, Germany 155
Naples, Italy 161
Nelson, 2nd Lt. Harold 122, 147
Nelson, Sgt Frederick 100
Newport News, Va. 164
Nosker, Capt. William 4, 49, 80, 81
Orange Club, Naples, Italy 153
Orbatello, Italy 143
Osijek, Yugoslavia 156
Perugia, Italy 65
Peninsula Base Section, Naples, Italy 163
Pickard, 2nd Lt. Harold 69
Ploesti, Romania 117, 118, 128, 133
Poggibonci, Italy 89
Porter, 2nd Lt. Fletcher 75
Postscript 171
Rasbach, 2nd Lt. David 139
Regensburg, Germany 91, 92, 94, 101
Resnick, 2nd Lt. Leonard 120
Rodgers, 2nd Lt. Dale 127
Rouse, 2nd Lt. Martin 124, 125, 126
Sao Luiz, Brazil 22
San Ceasaria a Mare 88
Schwecat, Austria 158
Sermersheim, 2nd Lt. Bernard 120, 140
Silvers, 2nd Lt. Henry 143
Simeria, Romania 153
Smith, Sgt. H. Carleton xiv, 6, 111
Smith, Sgt. Gilbert xiv, 72, 90
Sofia, Bulgaria 128
Stewart, 2nd Lt Warren 146
Steyr, Austria 97, 113

Taranto, Italy 45, 83
Temchulla, 2nd Lt. Frank 127
Thompkins, Capt Rex 60, 111
Tindouf, Morocco 37
Tope, Major William 62
Topeka Army Air Base, Kansas 15
Toulon, France 130, 157
Tunis, Morocco 41, 42
Udine, Italy 72
Van Sickle, 2nd Lt. Jay 133, 139
Wheeler, 2nd Lt. Hayward 75
Wiener-Neustadt, Austria 122, 150
Window 116
Wingfield, 2nd Lt. Harold 100
Winters, 2nd Lt. Robert 53
Wood, Jr. 1st Lt. John W. xiv, 27, 30, 86, 138, 158
Woods Chopper—B24-H #42-7750 13, 131, 158
47th Wing 60
98th Bomb Group 60
376th Bomb Group 60
449th Bomb Group 3, 60, 133
450th Bomb Group 60, 94, 95
718th Squadron 3, 133